FUN ON WHEELS

by

DAVE GARROWAY

Edited and revised by
COURTENAY EDWARDS

FOREWORD BY THE RT. HON.
VISCOUNT BRENTFORD

CHAIRMAN OF THE
AUTOMOBILE ASSOCIATION

Published in Collaboration with
THE AUTOMOBILE ASSOCIATION
by
FREDERICK MULLER LIMITED
LONDON

FIRST PUBLISHED IN 1962 IN GREAT BRITAIN BY
FREDERICK MULLER LIMITED
PRINTED AND BOUND BY COX & WYMAN LTD.

ACKNOWLEDGMENT

We are grateful to the Royal Society for the
Prevention of Accidents for their kind per-
mission to reproduce three of the illustrations
in this book

FOREWORD

Customs and habits are always changing but probably in no sphere have they changed more during the last fifty years than in motoring. We who were children then regarded a drive in the automobile as an adventure—and very often it was. When we were told to sit still in our seats we knew we jolly well had to, but the runs between stops, voluntary or enforced, were comparatively short.

Today however the car is universal and children accept it as a normal piece of family equipment; they bundle into it for a 200 mile run as cheerfully as we did for a 20 mile journey but they don't meet the same adventures. Children have not changed and without something to distract their minds they get bored and when bored in a motor car they are very quickly up to some antic which will distract the driver of the car from his all-important duty of keeping his attention on the road.

Lack of concentration on the part of drivers is one of the principal causes of road accidents and it is because the use of this book will help to keep the junior passengers amused and so contribute to greater safety on the roads that the A.A. has gladly associated itself with its production; but at the same time I am sure that it will also add to the joys of family motoring and bring happiness to many, both young and old.

Brentford.

CONTENTS

THE AGONY OF IT!

Nowadays more people are taking children on fairly long car trips than ever before—to the West Country, to Scotland, even to France and Italy—and I am sure most fathers have shared the agony of countless questions like "How many miles till we get there, Daddy?", "How far have we come now, Daddy?" or "Are we in Cornwall yet, Daddy?"

This book is an attempt to solve the problem of what to do with restless children when touring by car and I am deeply indebted to the Automobile Association for many helpful suggestions.

Fun on Wheels is an attempt to pass on to the general motoring public the benefit of research work which has enabled my own family to enjoy peaceful motoring; to have fun in the car as well as at journey's end.

We use many little tricks to break up a day's driving. For instance, I buy only two gallons of petrol at a time. This means that we stop more often to stretch our legs at filling-stations, and the children get a chance to run around for a few minutes.

I also try to maintain a flexible approach to the day's driving. I am not one of those drivers who keep strict schedules; go so many miles a day come hell or high water; and cannot eat until they reach such and such a town. This sort of driver considers the road something to be conquered rather than something to be enjoyed. We stop when the mood moves us. We stretch out on the grass while the kids work off surplus energy, and we do a lot of picnicking.

We've discovered that in all but the biggest cars it's a mistake to put anything inside except people. The children need all the room they can get for that wriggling and squirming which is an essential part of their existence. We put our luggage in the boot or on the roof rack. Inconvenient? A little, but that's nothing compared to the inconvenience of three children who sometimes are bored and restless.

These are the basic physical comforts we try to provide. Once we're sure of these, we try to plan activities—fun on wheels for the children.

Children over fourteen don't need these distractions. They can listen to the radio, talk, and even more important, they can stand a certain amount of boredom like an adult. I've written this book for people who travel with children under fourteen, children who easily become impatient, restless and complaining.

I've assembled a variety of games, puzzles, riddles and handicrafts to do while travelling in a car. Included are a few "nature games" designed for brief stops, but all the other games in this book can be played sitting down as you travel. They require little equipment or space. All you'll need are pencils, crayons, paper, blunt-ended scissors, paste or adhesive tape, a pack of cards, a draught-board and the desire to have fun. Adults can join in most of the games.

Singing songs and telling stories are also excellent diversions for children. Before we leave on a trip we gather up a few song books and story books.

I have no special skill as a leader of children, games master or recreation expert. Yet all that follows has worked for me. I think it will work for you, too.

I have imagined ours is a family of three children—David, about five, Michael about nine and Susan about twelve—so as to cover a fairly wide range of ages. My wife's name is Pam.

Don't try to work through the whole book at once. Browse gently through it, skip when you want to skip, then try a variety of suggestions: a quiz, a party game, a novelty draughts game, a few riddles and brain teasers. If the family doesn't show much enthusiasm for a game you pick, don't push it. Everybody's got to share the mood. Try things that are completely new to you. You'll find something that will intrigue everyone. Frankly, I have put things in this book that may sound rather silly, but which have given me personally a great deal of pleasure.

I

GAMES OF TRAVEL

W HEN YOU TAKE a long trip in a car, the simple act of looking can be the basis for a lot of car games. Some are based on number plates, some on remembering roadside scenes. Other games help a child learn to read maps or add to his knowledge of geography.

Under the heading of "Travel" I have also included the nature games we play when we stop to picnic.

"Looking" games are not for the driver. His job is to keep quiet and keep his eye on the road.

Road Sign Alphabet. This is a game for two, and any child who knows the alphabet can play.

One player watches the right side of the road, and the other the left. When a child sees the letter *A* in any word in a sign on his side, he calls out, "A". Then he looks for a *B*, and for each letter of the alphabet in turn. Allowing only one letter from any one sign, the child who first completes the alphabet wins the game. There are usually enough roadside signs to make the game workable.

Number-Plate Spelling. The purpose of this game is to pick a word and spell it out by finding the letters on the number plates of oncoming cars. Each player choose his word in advance and tells it to the others. Young children may pick simple three-letter words like "car", "cat", or "dog". Other children should choose longer, more difficult words, provided they are equal in length.

As we play it, each player takes an oncoming car in turn. Michael looks for the first letter of his word on the number plate of the first. Susan looks at the second car, Pam the third, and so on. (In theory, David, who cannot spell, is napping through all this.) Only one letter may be taken from any one number plate, and the letters must be found in the order of their appearance in the word. The number *O* may also be used as a letter. The first player to complete his word wins.

Number-plate spotting games of this type are best played when oncoming traffic is steady but spaced out.

Odd and Even Plates. Two players compete in this contest. While watching oncoming cars, one child tallies the number plates that end in odd numbers while his opponent scores those that end in even numbers. We usually set a goal of 25 to 50 points as the winning score, depending on how long the game seems to be holding interest.

Lucky Pairs. Assign each child a group of numbers he will watch for on the plates of oncoming cars. If

14

two children are playing, the first may look for 1,2,3,4, and 5, and the second for 6,7,8,9, and 0. With three children we divide it 1,2,3 for the first child, 4,5,6 for the second, and 7,8,9 for the third.

The children take turns in checking the plate of each oncoming car for pairs of any of their assigned number. The paired numbers must be together. Thus 55 would be good for one point, but 505 would not. The first player to get 10 points wins.

Highway Observation. This is a good game for country roads or secondary roads. We begin by making lists of commonly seen objects such as the following:

List One (for David)	List Two (for Michael)	List Three (for Susan)
Horse	Chickens	Cow
Pond	Brook	River
Bridge	Gravel road	Cinema
Sweetshop	Grocer's shop	Caravan
Bicycle	Postman	Aeroplane
Field of corn	Apple tree	Haystack
Any road sign	"Stop" sign	"For sale" sign
Red light	Wooden fence	Cemetery
Barn	Shutters	Weeping willow
Train	Guard's van	Tractor

Give each player one list and a pencil. Whenever the player sees an object on his list, he calls it out and checks it off. Pam and David are partners in this game. The first one to complete the list waves it in the air and calls, "Observation". He's the winner. As a prize you may give him anything from a biscuit to three years in a Swiss finishing school.

15

Guess what I saw. This is a simple "observation" game that even tots can play.

The idea is for one child to spot something along the road and for the other players to guess what he saw.

Michael begins the game by calling out, "Guess what I saw." Then he tells us how many letters are in the name of the object. (When David plays we sometimes help him with a whispered hint.) Then Michael gives a fairly vague clue, relating to size, colour or some other detail of the object. The other players must guess what the object is before I clock off two miles. If they fail to guess correctly, Michael gives them another clue, and so on, until someone names the correct object. That player becomes "It" and starts the game again.

Number-Plate Bingo. To start this game Pam gives each child a home-made Bingo board of nine squares. (Diagram below.) Players fill in double numbers of their own choice in each square. Then Pam calls out the last two numbers of the number

15	23	36
45	61	74
83	91	99

plates of oncoming cars. (If traffic is heavy, she calls out numbers from every fifth or tenth car.)

If a child's number is called, he draws a line through it on the board. The game continues until one youngster has crossed out three squares in a row, up, down, sideways, or diagonally. If the winner is Susan, she murmurs, "Number-Plate Bingo!" If it's Michael, he shrieks.

First Letters. Here's a game for children who have begun to learn to spell. Each child takes the initial of his first name. Now he must spot objects seen through the car window that begin with this initial. David looks for dairy farms, daisies, diesel trucks, etc. Susan looks for sidecars, sheep, signals, etc. The players write down their lists while I drive fifteen miles.

MAPS AND MARKERS

The youngster who is old enough to spell out place names, even with a little adult help, can get a lot of fun out of learning to read road maps. After you teach the children what the various map symbols stand for, what the scale of distance is, and how to locate different points, they should be able to do the following things:

1. Tell distances from one place to another.
2. Find historical sites, woods, National Trust property, etc.
3. Discover what kind of roads are indicated on the map: motorways, trunks roads, secondary roads, or unfenced tracks.
4. Locate airports, lakes, rivers, mountains, etc.

As children discover that road maps can change

from meaningless diagrams to interesting portraits of the country, they are ready to play "map games".

Six Towns. We always keep several copies of regional maps in the glove compartment. Pam gives the names of towns to the children. The first child to locate all six, and circle them with a coloured pencil, is the winner.

Total Distance. Here's a good arithmetic exercise that eats up time for the third- and fourth-formers. Get them to calculate the distance between three pairs of towns on their maps (and no peeping at the mileage charts). Then they must add up the three figures. We put a ten-minute time limit on this game. After that time we ask for the answer and the closest total, as indicated on the mileage chart, wins.

How many Routes? This one's for smaller children. Simply give them two towns fairly far apart on the map. You can even help them locate the towns. Then, with crayon, they must draw as many different routes between the two as they can. They may use any class of road.

Inching Along. When a child asks for the ninety-second time, "Are we there yet?", this game will give the answer. At the start of any trip, we give Michael and David a large-scale map. When we travel we use one route for going, and another for returning. Michael—and David to the best of his ability (which frequently means asking Pam or Susan)—draws the "going" route in red crayon, and the return route in green crayon.

Once we're on the road, we give Michael a black crayon, and at every stop we make, he uses it to mark the distance we have covered. This makes him a map expert, gives him a realistic estimate of time and distance, and stops him from asking every two seconds, "Are we there yet?"

How many People? As we drive through towns and cities each of us looks around, estimates the population and writes down the figure. When we leave the town we check the population figure shown in the A.A. Members' Handbook to see who came closest.

Road Signs. Some day even the smallest of your children is going to be behind the wheel of a car. He might as well start learning the road signs right away. The two- or three-year-old can begin to tell the difference between red and green lights, and to make his debut as a back-seat driver by calling out, "Red light! Stop!" or "Green light! Go!" Older children can learn the meaning of basic road signs as given in the Highway Code, such as those given below.

You will find this on the approaches to major roads. You must stop until it is safe to go on.

Note how the shape of this sign differs from the "Halt" sign. You could distinguish them even when covered with snow.

The triangle, which is always red, means danger. Make sure it is safe to cross.

This sign warns that the road bends sharply enough to demand special care.

This pictorial sign is specially popular with children. Look out for an ungated railway crossing.

Now tell me what these road markings mean : . . . .

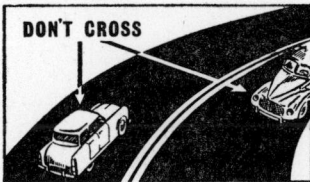

Answer : With double white lines you may cross them only if the broken line is nearer *your* side of the road. If both lines are solid neither traffic stream may cross.

Here is one of Britain's latest road signs. What is it?

Answer: It means what it says. Drivers must make the
road a clear way by not stopping or *parking*.

Where do you find this kind of sign?

Answer: On Britain's motorways. It shows you are
approaching a service area where you can: (1) Get
petrol; (2) Eat; (3) Buy a cup of tea; and (4) Park.

NATURE GAMES

When I travel with the family by car, I make frequent stops to let the children stretch their legs. As a matter of fact, I do the same myself. Two hours behind the wheel without a break is my limit. When we stop to picnic near some woods, we play a few simple nature games.

Bring it back. In a wooded area, it's our custom to take a fifteen- or twenty-minute walk through woods and fields. I bring along a list of simple nature objects that we are likely to come across, such as: yellow flower, grasshopper, frog, round pebble, acorn, oak leaf, bird's feather. Then we divide into teams to see who brings back the greatest number of things on the list.

I Hear. This is a resting game. We all sit quietly and write down the sounds we hear within a five- or ten-minute period. Sounds might include bird calls (properly identified), breeze in the trees, water flowing, a train whistle, a squirrel chattering, etc. David sits with Michael, who writes his list for him.

Guess the Petals. Pam has devised a number of simple lottery games that work nicely. She comes back from a walk with a flower, the type with well-defined petals, and asks each child, "How many petals has it got?" The closest guess wins the flower. She plays the same game with the leaves of a fern or the grains in an ear of corn.

My favourite is the ear of corn, because it always takes the children at least half an hour to count the grains after the guessing is over. Have *you* ever tried to count the grains on an ear of corn? It's practically impossible not to lose your place.

Tree Tag. This is a game for families of five or more. We play it with two teams of two players each, and Pam as referee. Each team picks the name of a tree common to the area. One might pick "birches", the other "elms". The teams face each other a few feet apart. Pam calls out the name of one of the trees. If she calls "Birches", the birch team must run to a birch tree while the elm team tries to tag them before they can reach it. If the birch team is tagged, the elm team wins a point. We play the game several times. In the long run each team has an equal number of tries. Highest score wins.

2

FUN FOR JUST A FEW

Y OU MAY BE surprised to discover that games you have played over cocktails and canapés are perfectly good for children over biscuits and milk. The following games are designed for two or three players.

Who Am I? Even David, the youngest in our family, can play "Who Am I?" The trick is simple. We select a new identity for him. We don't tell it to him, but we tell it to each other. Then David has to ask questions in the effort to determine who he is. He asks, "Am I a person?", "Am I an animal?", "Am I real?", "Am I in a story?"

By this time he knows the answer because we always decide that he is either Winnie the Pooh or Miss Johnson, his nursery-school teacher. Yet he always gets a kick out of the game.

With Michael, Susan, and ourselves, of course, we use far more difficult personalities. I may be Napoleon. I may even be Josephine, or even, despite Pam's jibes, Casanova.

In this game, the other players must answer each question with a "Yes", "No", or "I don't know". Whoever is "It" must ask his questions during five miles of travel, and then he has three guesses to discover the secret identity we've pinned on him.

Shopping on Account. This game was originally called "Pirate Treasure", but I like "Shopping on Account" better. Whoever is "It" begins by saying, "If I had an account at any shop in the world, I would buy . . ." Then he pauses and gives the other a vague hint: colour, weight, or some such quality. The others try to guess what it is, and if they do not come close, he gradually gives them more and more hints until someone guesses it correctly.

This game is very valuable for parents. It helps you find out what wheels are turning in those tousled little heads and gives useful pointers to remember at Christmas.

I'm Thinking of a Word. I participate in this game when Pam is driving. I announce, "I'm thinking of a word that rhymes with snow."

Then the children guess, running through "dough", "show", "blow", and others, until they finally hit on "crow". Whoever guesses correctly now has the privilege of thinking of a secret for the others to guess.

Twenty Questions. One of us writes down the name

of a physical object, anything at all from peanuts to plutonium. He folds the paper and puts it in his pocket. The other players take turns asking questions which help them find the identity of the object. These questions should be first gauged to determine the general nature and location of the object, and then narrow it down to more specific areas.

The player answers questions with a "Yes", "No", or "I don't know". Twenty questions are the limit. If a player guesses the secret object before the questions are used up, he becomes "It". Otherwise the original player shows what was on the paper, and starts the game again. With youngsters, pick simple objects.

I've seen this game carry us successfully through four towns, past twelve petrol stations, and around three domestic crises.

Animal, Vegetable, or Mineral. This is a form of "Twenty Questions", except that the player can use composite subjects. He can select something real or fictional, and it may be anything under the sun, provided that the other players have heard or read about it.

The player begins by giving the others a clue. If the subject belongs to, or is derived from, the animal kingdom, he tells them it is "animal". (This includes human beings.) If the subject is vegetable or plant, or made from a vegetable substance, he says, "vegetable". If it is mineral, he so identifies it. If it is any combination of animal, vegetable, or mineral, he must declare the combination.

Here are things we have used in this game:
Peter Pan (animal)

David's winter coat (animal and mineral—wool,
with metal buttons)
The walls of Jericho (mineral)
The whole wide world (animal, vegetable and
mineral)

In this form, you might have to allow thirty rather
than twenty questions. The secret subject may be
deceptively simple, like "Our coffee-cups at home",
but it may take just as many guesses to narrow it
down.

Continued Story. This is a stunt game for children
who have just started to talk, and children who can't
stop talking. Pam or I always join in this one. One
of us—let's say Susan—starts to tell a story. In the
middle, she suddenly breaks off. The next player
must pick it up immediately and keep it going. This
continues until each player has had a turn. The last
player has the moral responsibility to wind up the
tale with a grand exciting climax.

Once, playing this game, I began to tell the story of
Macbeth. I brought the story up to the murder of
Duncan. By the time it got to Michael, who was last,
Macbeth was marrying Little Red Riding Hood in
Buckingham Palace.

Ghost. If you know this game—and almost everyone
does—just skip ahead. It can be played with anyone
who can spell.

The object is to avoid being the person to complete
a word. Susan starts by saying a letter; Michael
adds a letter; and Pam tacks on another. As they
each do this they must have a possible word in mind
that begins with the letters already given. Let's say

Susan now adds another letter—but she has carelessly completed a four-letter word. Michael sings out, "That's a word!", and Susan is penalized by being given a *G*, the first step towards becoming a full-fledged GHOST. (If she loses again she would be a G-H, then a G-H-O, etc.) The first person to be a complete GHOST is the loser.

If a player thinks that the previous person to say a letter is bluffing (that is, he does not have a real word in mind but is just trying to avoid completing a word), that player may challenge. Should the previous person not have a genuine word in mind, he is given a letter towards GHOST; but if he does have a word, then the challenger is penalized.

When young children play, make it a rule that whenever a word of three or more letters is completed, someone is penalized. With older players the completed word must be four or five letters long.

It's best to have a pocket dictionary with you to settle arguments about tricky words.

Heads or Tails Ghost. This is plain old GHOST with an added twist. Any player may, in turn, add a letter to the end or the beginning of the word that is being formed. Instead of just saying the new letter, he must say it together with the other letters to indicate whether it fits at the beginning or end of the word.

Coffee-pot. This is an old stand-by with us. One of us covers up our ears (but not the driver). The rest decide on a secret verb. Perhaps they write it on a slip of paper and pass it round. Then the one who was left out of the secret begins the questioning, using the word "coffee-pot" instead of the mysterious verb.

"Do children coffee-pot?"

"Do you need special equipment to coffee-pot?"

"Have we coffee-potted yet on this trip?"

Sooner or later, the interrogator begins to get some clues. He is allowed three guesses at the correct word. If he wins, he may be allowed to be "It" again, although it's best to rotate.

Tea-kettle. This is a game of homonyms—words that sound alike, but may be spelled differently and have different meanings.

Pam begins by saying, "I went fishing yesterday, and took my tea-kettle with me."

Michael says, "It was tea-kettle good fun."

Susan joins in, "If I had a movie camera, I'd have taken a tea-kettle of you."

Meanwhile, I try to work out the meaning of tea-kettle, remembering that it must be a homonym. Finally, I realize that the key words are real and reel.

Other tea-kettle words that come easily to mind are: bore and boar; deer and dear; rain, reign, and rein; plane and plain; by and buy; see and sea.

Never Say It. We begin this simple conversation game by deciding among ourselves that a certain word, such as "I" or "No", must not be spoken. Then we start a general conversation in which we each try to trick the other into saying the forbidden word. Whenever this happens, the loser gets a penalty point. We talk for ten miles and after that the player with the fewest penalty points is the winner. Pam always tries to get "I" accepted as the penalty word. Children have an awfully tough time getting along without that word.

We have a variation on the game that makes it a little more difficult. Instead of picking a forbidden word, we pick a forbidden letter. Then Pam asks a question of each of the children in turn. The answers must be in a sentence of at least four words, none of which contains the forbidden letter. This game excludes David, who cannot spell, and is a little tough on Michael, who can spell but won't.

LIMBERING-UP GAMES

On long trips I have always noticed that what the children find most tiresome is their inability to move about freely.

Once when I found myself seriously wondering if the R.S.P.C.C. would be after me if I tied them all up, I realized I had let my feelings run away with me. What is needed are some physical games that can be played within the confines of a car.

Do This and Add Something. This is a little action game that Pam usually starts. She claps her hands several times. Then Susan claps her hands and then sneezes. Now Michael claps his hands, sneezes, and scratches his head. David, claps his hands, sneezes, scratches his head and stamps his feet.

Each player continues to add one action to those of the player before him. The last player to be able to repeat everything correctly and add a new action is the winner.

31

I'm Taking a Jet Plane. This is played like the previous game, but all in pantomime. The pantomime is confined to things the players might take with them on a jet plane. Pam could start by showing a suitcase. Susan could then pantomime a suitcase and an umbrella. Michael could add a fiddle, and David could add a Tommy-gun. Personally, I wouldn't let him on a jet plane with a Tommy-gun, but as long as it's pantomime, we're tolerant.

O'Grady Says. The O'Grady in question is a cousin of the Simon in "Simon says". Susan, being the oldest of the children, usually takes the part of O'Grady and lets Pam referee. Susan gives commands such as "O'Grady says bounce up and down". Michael and David must then obey immediately. But if she omits the phrase, "O'Grady says", they must not obey. Susan tries to think of as many different actions—clapping, stamping, nodding heads, wiggling knees, etc.—as are feasible in a car. The trick is to keep the commands coming fast.

Although you can give a penalty to the child who makes a mistake by not listening to the "O'Grady says", the main purpose of the game is to give the children exercise rather than eliminate them. We just try to keep the game going at a good pace, and we usually forget to keep score.

Rhythm Spelling. Older children enjoy this action-and-spelling game that stresses co-ordination. First let the children warm up for the game by clapping hands once against their own knees, then clapping hands together, and then snapping fingers. They

should do this in a steady rhythm, not too fast:
KNEES-HANDS-FINGERS, KNEES-HANDS-FINGERS.

The verbal action takes place on the finger-snapping beat.

Move from player to player in turn (Pam to Susan to Michael to David). The idea is to say a letter of the alphabet on *your* snap, and to have the next player say a word beginning with that letter, on the *next* snap. Then he says a letter, and the next player must say a word beginning with that letter. All right. Start the rhythm:

CLAP KNEES! CLAP HANDS! SNAP! (Pam says "R".)
CLAP KNEES! CLAP HANDS! SNAP! (Susan says "Rabbit".)
CLAP KNEES! CLAP HANDS! SNAP! (Susan says "B".)
CLAP KNEES! CLAP HANDS! SNAP! (David says "B-b-buhh!")

Because David was unable to say a word in time (he's a bit young for the game) we give him a penalty point, but we don't tell him about it.

Start the game slowly, then speed it up as the players get the knack. Whoever has fewest misses after several minutes or miles have gone by is the winner.

SILLY SEASON GAMES

Here's our collection of relatively active little stunts and contests that help relieve physical fatigue.

Sixes and Noughts. Ask the children to make a "six" in the air with their right hands. Then have them make a clockwise circle, or "nought", on the floor with their left feet. Next they must try to do both actions simultaneously.

Rub and Rub. Ask the children to rub their chests with one hand in a clockwise motion while they rub their stomachs with the other hand in a counter-clockwise motion.

Rub and Pat. This combines a circular rub of the chest with one hand and a pat of the stomach with the other.

Opposites. Susan faces Michael. Susan is the "actor" and Michael is the "mirror". Michael's job is immediately to imitate or "reflect" the various actions that Susan performs. After a while they change over.

Make 'em Laugh. At some point in his life almost every child plays this game spontaneously. It's simple. One child faces another, and by using silly gestures or by laughing himself, he tries to make the other laugh. A variation is "Make 'em yawn". By yawning himself, one child tries to make his opponent yawn.

Living Nursery Rhymes. Hand movements to nursery rhymes provide action for children that can easily be kept within bounds.

Even older children like to join in, trying to make their miming more appropriate or inventive. For example, "Sing a song of sixpence" could go something like this:

Sing a song of sixpence,

A pocket full of rye (hands in pockets)

Four and twenty blackbirds (hold up fingers to number two and four)

Baked in a pie (pretend to make pie).

When the pie was opened (cut it open)

The birds began to sing (imitate bird song)

Wasn't that a dainty dish to set before a king? (Put dish on table).

And so on . . . .

Many other well-known nursery rhymes lend themselves to this treatment.

Birds and Animals. Pam tells a story with plenty of animal and bird names in it. Every time the name of a bird is mentioned, the children must remain silent and flap their hands to imitate wings.

When the name of an animal crops up they must keep perfectly still and try to reproduce the sound the animal makes.

Of course, if they move when they should speak or make a noise when hand-flapping is called for, they are "out".

3

WORD GAMES

W ORD GAMES ARE probably our favourite form of recreation inside the travelling car. They take a fairly long period of time and they hold the interest more consistently than stunt games.

Most of these games have many possible solutions. Half the fun comes when the work is over and we compare results. They're designed for all children who can spell and write, at whatever level. All you need is paper and pencil.

Alphabet Story. Allow eight to ten miles for each player to write a story of exactly twenty-six words. But each word of this story must start with a successive letter of the alphabet from A to Z. The most imaginative story wins. Here's one that Susan wrote:

Apple Blossoms Come Down Every Friday. Going Home in Jogging Knocking Lorry Makes Naughty Oliver Pretend Quick Recovery. Still, To Use Violins Without Xylophone Yields Zest.

If the game is too difficult, let the children use pocket dictionaries, or you can divide up and play teams.

Alphabet Travelling. This game demands some knowledge of geography. One child picks a destination and something to do when he gets there, starting with the letter A. For instance, Michael says, "I'm going to Ashford." Another child must ask "What will you do when you get there?" He must respond in words beginning with A, such as, "Act afraid."

Then Pam announces that she is going to Birmingham. Susan asks what she will do and she replies, "Buy beautiful bicycles."

So it goes down the alphabet.

Geography. Give each child paper and pencil. On the left of the paper print the word "geography" vertically down the page. At a signal each player writes the name of a country, county, or town after each letter in the word. For example:

G   Glasgow
E   Estonia
O   Oxfordshire

The player who finishes first, or who has written down the largest number of correct names within a time limit, wins.

First Names. Ask the children to pick out a first name that is fairly long, and write it down, crossing out any duplicate letters. Under each letter of the name, they must now write other first names that start with the same letter. Try "Robert".

R	O	B	E	(R) T
Rex	Ophelia	Barry	Edith	Tom
Randolph	Oscar	Barbara	Edwin	Terry
Richard	Olive	Billy	Edward	Tina
Robin	Oliver	Bert	Evelyn	Theodore
Rita	Olga	Bertha	Esther	Tessa
Renee			Elsie	

We play this game for about eight miles, after which we see who has the most names on his list.

Fill in the Words. We begin by picking any fairly long word. Then we write the word vertically, just as in "Geography" down the left side of the paper. On the other side, we write it vertically again, but this time backwards. Let's say were using the word DEMOCRACY. On the right side of the paper we would have YCARCOMED. Now the trick is to fill in words of any length beginning with the letter on the left and ending with the letter on the right. Suppose we stick with DEMOCRACY:

```
D  R  A  Y
E  P  I  C
M  A  L  A  R  I  A
O  D  O  U  R
C  O  M  I  C
R  A  D  I  O
A  L  B  U  M
C  R  A  N  E
Y  A  R  D
```

38

This is a ten-mile game for us, after which we see who has been able to complete the list. When we have young children with us we let them use words of any length, but the older children must have words of at least four letters.

Sometimes we play this in teams rather than as individuals. (David always does better on a team.)

Find the Simile. A Simile is a figure of speech in which something is compared (using "like" or "as") with something of a different kind. But let's not get complicated. We simply ask each other for the word that obviously fits at the end of these incompleted similes:

> Bitter as........ (gall)
> Blind as .... (a bat)
> Clean as .... (a whistle)
> Cold as .... (ice)

And so on, and so on. You know thousands. Dead as a doornail. Shy as a violet. Cool as a cucumber. Ugly as sin. Honest as the day is long.

Sometimes I write these lists of similes in advance, distribute them among the children, and let them ask each other.

The Missing Word. This game is similar to the one above. I prepare a list of familiar paired phrases and expressions, and ask the child to complete them. They are phrases we all know and use (to death), such as:

Ham and . . . . (eggs)
Peaches and . . . . . . (cream)
Jack and . . . . (Jill)
Needle and . . . . . . (thread)

You'll know lots.

Scrambled Animals. This is one of the games I always prepare in advance. I distribute sheets of paper containing the pictures of ten different animals. Opposite each picture, but not in the same order, I write their names, thoroughly scrambled. The children have to unscramble the names and fit them to the proper picture.

word		*picture*	
1.	ORSEH	A.	Squirrel
2.	WOC	B.	Goat
3.	KONEYD	C.	Lion
4.	ATC	D.	Elephant
5.	QUIRSREL	E.	Cat
6.	TOGA	F.	Cow
7.	MELCA	G.	Horse
8.	IOLN	H.	Tiger
9.	REGIT	I.	Donkey
10.	HANTELPE	J.	Camel

Scrambled Cities. Here we use world-famous cities with their names scrambled, and we ask the children to work out which each one is.

1.	NODONL	(London)
2.	ISRAP	(Paris)
3.	WEN OKRY	(New York)
4.	OSOL	(Oslo)
5.	LUTTACAC	(Calcutta)
6.	SCOMWO	(Moscow)

7. TONGINHAWS   (Washington)
8. KOYOT   (Tokyo)
9. LERBIN   (Berlin)
10. IOR ED ANJOIRE   (Rio de Janeiro)

Oddmen. Each of the following sentences contains a word that does not fit in context. The object of the game is to locate the "oddman" and by rearranging its letters spell out a word that makes sense in the context. For instance, in the statement, "They took a steamship across the canoe," the "oddman" is the word "canoe". It should be changed to spell "ocean".

Try your hand at solving the following "oddmen". If you don't solve all of them, you'll find the answers below.

1. Detectives often crate missing persons.
2. I'll have a lemon and mile soda.
3. When the fat lady stepped on the laces, she shuddered.
4. Most blackboards are made out of steal.
5. You need a sharp knife properly to crave turkey.
6. To cheat is a teacher's job.
7. He fell in the ditch and was covered with miles.
8. The fellow was a bore—an absolute cold.
9. Pity the poor open of Mexico.

The solutions are below:

1.	Crate—trace	6.	Cheat—teach
2.	Mile—Lime	7.	Miles—slime
3.	Laces—scale	8.	Cold—clod
4.	Steal—slate	9.	Open—peon
5.	Crave—carve		

Add a Letter. This is "oddmen" with an added element. I give the children one word. They must add a letter to it, then rearrange it to fit a definition. I might say to Michael, "Add an *e* to cars and get fright." The answer is scare. Ready? Add a letter to:

lend, and get a careful mixture   (blend)
scow, and get some black birds   (crows)
beam, and get a yellowish resin used to make beads   (amber)
grin, and get wheat or barley   (grain)
steer, and get the latest hi-fi equipment
          (stereo)
lean, and get something found in geometry
          (angle)

Word to Word. Here's a somewhat trickier word game which you may know under the name of "Changelings". The children must move from the first word given to the last, changing one letter each time, and always spelling a word, in the number of steps required.

I might say, "Michael, move from *crop* to *tool* in three steps." And Michael, bright child, would answer CROP, COOP, COOL, TOOL.

Here are others:

Sick to *bark* in three steps. (SICK, SACK, BACK, BARK)
Scar to *beam* in three steps. (SCAR, SEAR, BEAR, BEAM)
Door to *roam* in four steps. (DOOR, DOOM, LOOM, LOAM, ROAM)

Sing to *vale* in four steps. (SING, SANG, SANE, VANE, VALE)

Dire to *fond* in four steps. (DIRE, FIRE, FORE, FORD, FOND)

OTHER WORD GAMES

Hidden Words. This game may be a daily feature in your newspaper. Simply take a fairly long word and see how many four- or five-letter words you can make up, using the letters found in it. (You may not use the letters more often than they appear in the word.)

We play this game in teams and it's usually good for ten to fifteen miles of peace. Let's say we look for five-letter words hidden in EXPLORATIONS. We get: extra, plate, opera, store, slain, panel, stair, trail, and so on. I managed to find thirty-four word in EXPLORATIONS in ten minutes. I'm sure that a dictionary would help me find another twenty.

The game works best with words of ten or twelve letters that have a minimum of three vowels.

Spelling Bee. A spelling bee can be lots of fun if you run it flexibly, gearing the contest to the age of the contestants. We don't even bother with a list. We just pick the words out of a newspaper or magazine.

We organize our spelling bees by giving each one a turn. If one person misses, the next person gets a crack at the same word, and can pick up a point. Sometimes we play the front seat against the back seat, and if one team misses, the other team tries the same word.

We have a variation on the spelling bee that's a favourite with us. When any of us must spell a word containing the letter *a*, we do not say the letter *a* aloud. Instead, we lift our right hand to our right ear and then drop it again. We are not permitted to say *t* aloud either. Instead we must lift our left hand and touch our left ear. If we fail to make these gestures we lose a point even though we may have spelled the word correctly.

Ible or Able? This is our *ible-able* spelling bee—the one I always lose. It's based on that old teaser—does a word end in *ible* or *able*? Ask the players to write these words down, and then complete them with the correct suffix:

(correct answers)

1.	Admir	ABLE	8.	Perish	ABLE
2.	Practic	ABLE	9.	Convert	IBLE
3.	Indel	IBLE	10.	Vener	ABLE
4.	Aud	IBLE	11.	Compat	IBLE
5.	Credit	ABLE	12.	Excus	ABLE
6.	Intellig	IBLE	13.	Charit	ABLE
7.	Inevit	ABLE	14.	Infall	IBLE
			15.	Mov	ABLE

Group Limericks. Here's our last word game—group limericks. The first player makes up a first line, and then each player adds a line in turn. It needn't make much sense, but it must rhyme properly. A player who cannot add a line in two miles of travel must retire from the game, and so it goes until only one person, the champion, remains.

(I always beat David at this game but he maintains it is because I am older than he is.)

Here's one:

"There was a young man from New York
Who ate with a knife, not a fork,
He cut up a worm
And detected a germ
And let out a horrible squawk."

4

CHESTNUTS OLD AND NEW

HERE'S A COLLECTION of riddles, puzzles, pencil-and-paper games and challenges that will brighten odd moments while your car purrs along the highway.

You'll remember some of these chestnuts from your school days. They stay alive for ever, and my children are always coming home with riddles that I first learned in the first form. But you'll find some new ones among the old.

Grin and Bear It.

Do you remember these riddles?

What can you give someone and still keep for yourself? (A cold)

Why do hens lay eggs only in the daytime? (Because at night they become roosters.)

How can you carry water in a sieve? (Freeze it first.)

What is a cow after she is five years old? (Six years old.)

What is black and white and read all over? (A newspaper.)

What has eyes and cannot see? (A potato.)

What has four wheels and flies? (A dustcart.)

What has legs and cannot walk? (A table.)

Why is Ireland about to become the wealthiest country in the world? (Because its capital is always doublin'.)

The more you take away, the bigger it grows. What is it? (A hole.)

What has pains (panes) and doesn't ache? (A window.)

Where does Friday come before Thursday? (In the dictionary.)

What has six legs, two heads, and two arms? (A man on horseback.)

Why do Eskimoes cry so often? (Because they must have their daily blubber.)

What is the difference between here and there? (The letter "t".)

What is bought by the yard but worn by the foot? (A rug.)

What has holes and yet holds water? (A sponge.)

What is a question that you cannot honestly answer "no" to? (What does "y-e-s" spell?)

What international disaster could be caused by a housewife who dropped a dish on Christmas Day? (It would be the downfall of Turkey, the overthrow of Greece, and the destruction of China.)

Why is a person's nose in the middle of his face? (Because it's the scenter.)

Who was the smallest man in the world? (The Roman soldier who went to sleep on his watch.)

Why was the little raspberry worried? (Because her Mum and Dad were in a jam.)

Why are the people who live in big cities most ignorant? (Because that's where the population is most dense.)

Three men fell in the ocean, but only two got their hair wet. Why? (Because the third man was bald.)

And didn't we all grow up with this one?

> England, Ireland, Scotland, Spain,
> All fell down in a shower of rain;
> Spell that in four letters.

The answer? "T-h-a-t."

PUZZLES UNLIMITED

Here are some puzzles that take a little thinking about:

Rock in the Cellar. Mr. and Mrs. Jones wanted to deepen the cellar in their home. They hired a contractor, Willie Diggem, to do the job. Everything went smoothly until Willie uncovered a huge rock under the surface, right in the middle of the cellar. It was too big to be taken up the steps. Willie couldn't blast it without blowing the house down. Chipping at it would take too long. What were the Joneses to do? Move? Give up the idea? They stood next to Willie's truck, talking it over, when they caught sight of their dog. The dog gave them the answer. What did they do with the huge boulder?

Solution: The dog had been gnawing a bone. Then he dug a hole and buried it in the ground. This was the perfect answer. Willie dug a deep hole in the cellar and buried the tremendous rock in it. Then he carried out the earth the rock had displaced and finished the job.

Low Bridge. A big lorry stopped in front of a railway bridge bearing the sign: "Low Bridge Clearance, 11 feet, 1 inch". The lorry stood exactly 11 feet, 2 inches high. The driver had no alternate route to take. He didn't want to tear the roof off his lorry. Cars piled up behind him and trapped him. How did he get through?

Solution: He let a little air out of each tyre until the lorry sank down one inch. He drove through slowly, and then stopped at the next petrol station for some air.

Silk Stockings. This is a quick one. A woman has fifty silk stockings. Twenty-five are light tan, and twenty-five are a rich brown shade. She sends her blind maid to bring her a pair. What is the smallest number of stockings the blind maid must bring to be sure there is one matched pair?

Solution: Three. There might be one of each colour if there were only two. But the third one would have to make a pair.

Captain Harrington's Bear. The great explorer, Captain Harrington, was trampling over difficult terrain when he spied a bear. The captain checked his compass, then lifted his rifle and aimed due south. The bear began to run due east. The captain continued to aim due south, and fired. His shot killed the bear. What colour was the bear?

Solution: The bear was white. Captain Harrington was at the North Pole where every compass direction is south. Only if he were there could he shoot an eastward-running bear by aiming at a south compass point. The bear must have been a polar bear, which comes in only one colour.

Settlers and Indians. This, I understand, is a classic, and it is new to me every time I do it because I always forget the solution. Put a piece of paper on the car seat or on a suitcase. Draw a line across it to represent a river. On one side place three small sticks and three pebbles. The sticks are Indians, the pebbles are settlers. The problem is to transfer all six to the other side of the river in a canoe. Any two may cross at a time, but at least one must return to bring the canoe back to the others. And, most important, there must never be more Indians than settlers left together on either side of the river.

Solution: Two Indians go over. One comes back and takes another Indian over. One Indian returns. Two settlers now go over. A settler and an Indian now come back. Two settlers cross over. One Indian returns. Two Indians go over. One Indian returns and takes the final Indian over with him.

Count the Ducks. This one is a little easier. When someone asked a farmer how many ducks he had in the barnyard, he answered, "As they ran towards the pond I saw one duck in front of two ducks, one duck behind two ducks, and one duck between two ducks." What was the smallest number of ducks the farmer could have had?

Solution: Three ducks, one in front of another in a line.

Twins We're Not. Immigration officials interviewed two young Swedes as they stepped off the boat. An officer asked one boy his name. "Sven Johnson." He asked the other boy his name. "Lars Johnson." "Are you brothers?" asked the officer. "Yes," they said, "We're brothers." When the officer asked the date of their birth, they both replied, "November 20, 1946." "Then you're twins," said the officer. Both boys disagreed. "We're not twins," they said. "But," said the officer, "if you are brothers and were born on the same day, you *must* be twins." Was the officer right?

Solution: The boys were telling the truth. They had left behind a third brother, Tor, also born on the same day. They were TRIPLETS.

Mixed-up Relatives. At family gatherings, I can never trace relationships beyond first cousins. See if you can untangle the following mixed-up relatives. What relation to you is:

1. Your uncle's father's only grandchild? (Yourself)
2. Your sister's father's stepson's mother? (Your stepmother)
3. Your aunt's mother's father's wife? (Your great-grandmother)

4. Your brother-in-law's wife's grandmother's husband? (Your grandfather)
5. Your father's uncle's brother's sister? (Your great-aunt)
6. Your sister-in-law's father-in-law's grandson? (Your nephew)
7. Your brother's son's sister's mother? (Your sister-in-law)

Light in the Dark. A storm cuts off your electricity and you are without lights. You search the cupboards and find nine little candles. Each candle will burn for just one hour. However, you can melt down the candle ends and make new candles; it takes three ends to make one new candle. How many hours of candlelight will you have?

Solution: Thirteen. The original nine candles burn nine hours. You melt down their ends and get three candles that burn three hours. This leaves you with three ends that make one more candle, and one more hour of light.

PENCIL AND PAPER GAMES

Noughts and Crosses. I don't suppose there's anyone in the world who doesn't know how to play this game, but just in case, here it is.

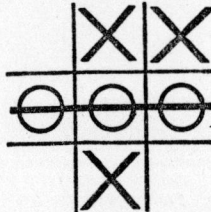

The game is played on a piece of paper with four intersecting lines. The first player makes an *0* in any box. His opponent then marks an *X* in any other box. The purpose is to get three *0*s or *X*s in a straight line, across, up or down, or diagonally. Players draw their marks in turn until one player has won or all the boxes are filled. Then they try again, taking turns in who goes first, since first move in this game is an advantage.

Gomuku. This is a Japanese version of Noughts and Crosses, and I'm told people sit up all night playing it.

Draw a grid of nineteen vertical lines intersecting nineteen horizontal lines. The diagram below

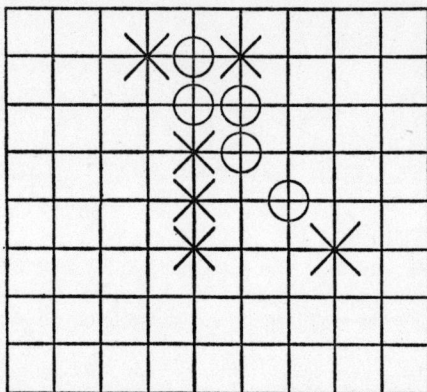

shows only the upper left-hand corner of this. This is how the Japanese play, adding more lines only as needed. Two players take turns making *X*s or *0*s on the intersections of the lines, *not* inside the squares. The purpose is to get five *X*s or *0*s in a straight line in any direction. It's a sort of large-size Noughts and Crosses.

The contest continues till one person wins or all the intersections are filled up.

Money Words. This is a simple game for youngsters, but it's enough to immobilize them for at least fifteen minutes. Buy a few copies of the same newspaper. Give the children a pencil and identical sheets from the newspapers. Each child draws a circle around every word on the page, back and front, that relates to money, such as "pay", "pounds", "interest", "loans", etc. When the time is up, we count the number of legitimate tallies.

You may find the financial pages too crammed with money terms. Another good subject is travel.

Doodles. The trick in these is to copy the diagrams below in one continuous line, without crossing a

line, taking pencil off the paper, or going over any line twice. First we let the children copy the diagrams exactly on their own sheets of paper, and then try to solve them.

Number Labyrinth. I ask Pam to write twenty or twenty-five pairs of numbers on a large sheet of paper. She separates the numbers as in the diagram below. She writes two of each number, two 1s, two 2s, etc.

Now the children take turns in drawing lines that connect the pairs of numbers. A player may not draw his line *through* any other line on the paper, or touch any other number. It's easy at the start, but it grows more difficult as the game progresses. Players drop out when they can no longer draw a connecting line. The last player to draw a successful line wins.

Don't forget to make the drawing on a large sheet of paper.

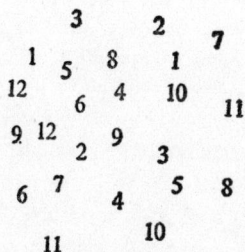

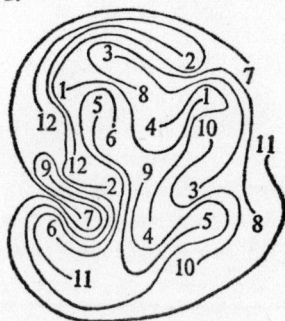

CHALLENGES

"Challenges" are really stunts that parents challenge youngsters to accomplish, or do themselves. Each is based on a little trick. For example:

Elastic Ring. When we are relaxing after a picnic lunch, I remove my ring, hold it up, and announce to three suspicious children that I can push a half-crown through it without breaking it.

They know enough not to bet. They know there's a trick involved, but they don't know what it is, and that's all that counts. To prove my point I take a half-crown, place it against the ring, slip my finger-tip through the ring, and push the half-crown.

They protest that I'm not doing what I said I could do. I remind them that all I said was that I could push a half-crown through a ring. And I did just that.

Name in One Letter. Now it is Pam's turn to be the wizard. She announces that she can write her name in one letter. The children brood over this for three or four minutes, and finally challenge her to do it. She takes a pencil and a piece of paper and draws a large single letter, usually an *O* or a *D*. Inside the *O* or *D* she writes "Pamela".

It's not quite Houdini, but it's a start.

Speedy Scribbling. About three of these is all we can bear, so here's the third. Susan tells Michael, "I can write faster than you, no matter how fast you can write." Anything that concerns speed is a challenge to Michael. Both he and Susan grab pencil and paper. I yell, "Go!" Both of them write furiously. But while Michael is writing whatever comes into his head, Susan is writing the phrase, "Faster than you." She has done exactly what she said she could do. She is writing "Faster than you," no matter how fast Michael is writing.

Mysterious Handkerchief. With this trick you can easily catch quite a lot of people. Take three handkerchiefs, two white ones and a coloured one (a scarf will do). Knot the two white ones together. Tie the coloured one to one end of a white one. Then challenge any child (or adult) to put the coloured handkerchief between the two white ones without untying the knots that connect them.

Solution: Just make a third knot so that all three handkerchiefs are tied together in a circle. The coloured one will now be between the two white ones, and you have undone no knots.

Magic Postcard. When Pam takes over the driving, our children concentrate their attack on me. I announce that I can put myself through a postcard. Then I take a postcard, or a piece of heavy paper cut down to postcard size, and fold it in half down its length. Next I take a pair of scissors and, starting at the folded edge close to one end of the card, I cut almost all the way through. Then, about an eighth of an inch below this cut and starting at the open edge, I cut almost through to the folded edge. I keep this up, cutting alternately at the folded edge and then the straight edge, until I've gone all the way down the length of the card. The last cut should start at the folded edge.

Next I cut each joined connection down the centre of the unfolded card, except the first and last connections. Then I carefully unfold the postcard without forcing it. I am left with a large paper circle that even I have no difficulty slipping through.

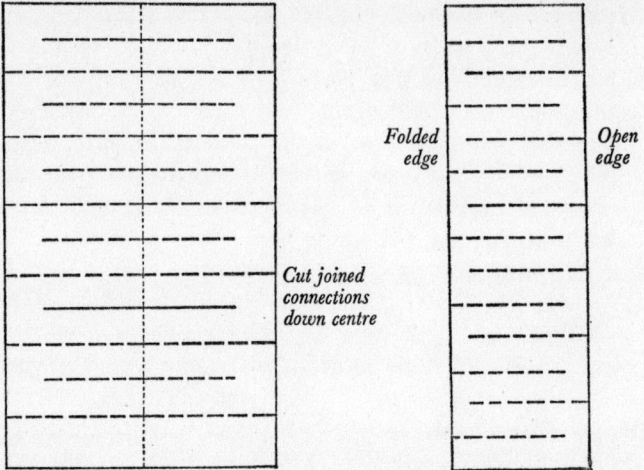

Folded edge

Open edge

Cut joined connections down centre

5

TEST YOUR BRAIN POWER

Quizzes have long been one of the oldest sources of group entertainment.

Here is a collection of them. I've tried to pick those that are on a child's level, and the subjects cover animals, sports, famous personalities, geography, history and astronomy. I'm presenting the easy ones first and going on to others that are a little more difficult.

Sometimes we're quite informal about the quizzes, tossing out the questions to anyone who can answer. At other times we make it a contest between the Front Seat and the Back Seat. In the latter case, teams answer in turn. If you want to score, give one point for the correct answer, and a —1 for an incorrect answer.

What is It. Very young children will respond to the following quiz:

Can you identify these fourteen animals, including birds, fish and reptiles? The answers are in brackets.

1. This little animal with large ears loves carrots. (Rabbit)
2. This slippery fish looks something like a snake. (Eel)
3. This sea-going mammal is the largest of all living creatures. (Whale)
4. This lovely pink bird, common on some African lakes, sleeps on one leg. (Flamingo)
5. Touching the bumpy skin of this little creature was said to cause warts. (Toad)
6. This animal builds dams across streams by gnawing down trees. (Beaver)
7. This big, sharp-toothed fish is the terror of ship-wrecked sailors. (Shark)
8. This tiny bird drinks the nectar of flowers and moves so fast you can hardly see his wings. (Hummingbird)
9. This black-and-white striped animal can produce a powerful scent to protect itself. (Skunk)
10. This furry little animal usually flies in the dark. (Bat)
11. This animal stores nuts for the winter. (Squirrel)
12. This creature has many sharp prickles as its protection. (Hedgehog)
13. This big bird can't fly but runs as fast as a horse. (Ostrich)

14. This slender cat looks like a leopard and is used by Indian princes to help them hunt. (Cheetah)

World of Sports. Here's one for some girls and all boys—a sports quiz. Give them this list of sports terms and let them write the game with which each term is associated. Answers are in brackets:

1.	Maiden over	(Cricket)
2.	Rowlock	(Rowing)
3.	Shuttlecock	(Badminton)
4.	Fairway	(Golf)
5.	Slalom	(Skiing)
6.	Double fault	(Tennis)
7.	Chukker	(Polo)
8.	Technical K.O.	(Boxing)
9.	Puck	(Ice Hockey)
10.	Figure eight	(Figure skating)
11.	Lap chart	(Motor Racing)
12.	Line-out	(Rugby Football)
13.	Off-side	(Football)
14.	Bully-off	(Hockey)

Favourite Foods. Here I've devised a little quiz (it's easy to invent your own) to test the children's knowledge of zoology. It's just a list of foods, and the children are supposed to tell what animals habitually eat these foods. The answers are in the opposite column.

FISH	Seal, cat, otter, etc.
ACORNS	Squirrel
LETTUCE	Rabbit, guinea pig
HAY	Cow or horse

BANANAS	Monkey
INSECTS	Spider, bird
HONEY	Bear
FIELD MICE	Cat, fox, owl, other birds
EARTHWORM	Robin, other birds
PEANUTS	Elephant, squirrel.

Naturally, there are other possibilities for each of these.

County Neighbours. Sitting at the wheel, after a period of relative quiet that now seems to be ending with a small explosion, I call out, "Susan, I am Surrey," and we have started to play "County Neighbours". Susan, Michael and David (prompted by Pam) quickly start naming counties that border on Surrey. Whoever gives the most correct answers wins, and he becomes a county.

After each game we consult the map. Half the fun of this game is discovering how many misconceptions all of us have about the geography of the British Isles.

Here are some samples:

SURREY: Kent, Sussex, Hampshire, Berkshire, Middlesex, Greater London.
WARWICKSHIRE: Northamptonshire, Oxfordshire, Gloucestershire, Worcestershire, Staffordshire, Leicestershire.
WESTMORLAND: Lancashire, Cumberland, Durham, Yorkshire.

Animal Babies. See if your children know what the young of the following animals and birds are called. The answers are in brackets.

1. HEN (Chick)	8. SHEEP (Lamb)
2. SEAL (Calf)	9. LION (Cub)
3. FROG (Tadpole)	10. SWAN (Cygnet)
4. CAT (Kitten)	11. WHALE (Calf)
5. DOG (Puppy)	12. BEAR (Cub)
6. DEER (Fawn)	13. GOOSE (Gosling)
7. MARE (Filly or foal)	14. DUCK (Duckling)

What's the Country? Here's a little game that helps children get a sense of the world they live in. It's based on the unique customs, habits, or features of various countries. The answer to each of these questions is a nation.

1. Where is the home of the Pyramids?
2. Where do they ride reindeer?
3. Where do they make tea in samovers?
4. Where are the fjords, or narrow sea inlets?
5. Where do they eat a food called poi?
6. Where do they do the Highland Fling?
7. Where are gondolas used for transport?
8. Where do primitive bushmen still live?
9. Where do men wear a fez?
10. Where do they charm cobras?
11. Where is the llama used as a beast of burden?
12. Where do they dance with castanets?
13. Where do they eat spaghetti?
14. Where does the koala bear live?
15. Where do they live in snow houses called igloos?

Answers: 1. Egypt; 2. Lapland; 3. Russia; 4. Norway and other Scandinavian countries; 5. Hawaii; 6. Scotland; 7. Venice; 8. Australia;

63

9. Turkey and other countries in North Africa and the Middle East; 10. India; 11. Peru and other South American countries in the Andes Mountains; 12. Spain, and other countries settled by Spaniards; 13. Italy; 14. Australia; 15. Wherever Eskimoes live.

Above or Below? This game is aimed at the younger of the younger set. I give them a list of common garden vegetables. Next to each vegetable they must write "above" or "below", depending on whether the edible part of the vegetable grows above or below the ground. The answers are on the right.

1. CARROTS (below)

2. ASPARAGUS (above)

3. CELERY (above)

4. TURNIPS (below)
5. CORN (above)
6. BEETROOT (below)
7. RADISHES (below)

8. TOMATOES (above)

9. CUCUMBERS (above)

10. POTATOES (below)

11. PARSNIPS (below)
12. LETTUCE (above)
13. RHUBARB (above)

Who Was That Lady I Saw You With Last Night? This is an animal game which Pam and I usually give orally. We ask one of the children, "Mr. Rooster, who was that lady I saw you with last night?" Mr. Rooster is supposed to answer "Hen," the female of the species. And round we go, with all the animals we can think of. Here's a list of male animals with their female counterparts:

1. ROOSTER	(Hen)	7. GANDER	(Goose)
2. BOAR	(Sow)	8. FOX	(Vixen)
3. TIGER	(Tigress)	9. BUCK	(Doe)
4. BULL	(Cow)	10. ELEPHANT	(Cow)
5. RAM	(Ewe)	11. STALLION	(Mare)
6. TOMCAT	(Tabby)	12. DRAKE	(Duck)

You can throw in a little additional information and make yourself a fount of wisdom by informing the children that a male fox is called a *dog*, and a male elephant is called a *bull*.

Nursery Headlines. Here's a quiz based on nursery and Mother Goose rhymes. I call out one of the following headlines, and ask the children in turn to tell me what nursery rhyme it refers to:

1. YOUNG SHEEP TRAILS GIRL TO SCHOOL.
2. BLIND RODENTS ATTACK FARMER'S WIFE.
3. SPIDER TERRORIZES SMALL GIRL.
4. PET STARVES AS OLD WOMAN RUNS OUT OF FOOD.
5. MISSING SHEEP REPORT HOME.
6. STEALER OF KISSES ESCAPES.
7. HIGH WIND THROWS INFANT FROM TREE CRADLE.
8. RETAILER DENIES CUSTOMER'S APPEAL FOR PASTRY.
9. KING'S MEN FAIL TO REVIVE VICTIM OF FALL.
10. TIME SIGNAL PANICS MICE.

Answers: 1. Mary Had a Little Lamb; 2. Three Blind Mice; 3. Little Miss Muffet; 4. Old Mother

Hubbard; 5. Little Bo-Peep; 6. Georgie-Porgie; 7. Rockabye, Baby; 8. Simple Simon; 9. Humpty-Dumpty; 10. Hickory-Dickory-Dock.

Animal Mortgages. The title of the game is a little misleading. The purpose of the quiz is simply to tell what the homes of various animals are called. It's been my habit to put the question in this form: "On what is Mr. Eagle paying off his first mortgage?" The names of the animals' homes are in brackets.

1.	EAGLE	(Eyrie)
2.	BEE	(Hive)
3.	CHICKEN	(Coop)
4.	HORSE	(Stable)
5.	PIGEON	(Dovecote)
6.	PIG	(Sty)
7.	RABBIT	(Burrow, hutch, or warren)
8.	SHEEP	(Fold or pen)
9.	MOLE	(Tunnel)
10.	WASP	(Nest)
11.	BEAVER	(Lodge or den)
12.	LION	(Den or lair)

In a quiz like this save the easy ones (bee, chicken, etc.) for the smaller children.

Around the World in Ten Minutes. This quiz is based on natural and man-made wonders of the world. Its purpose is to identify the countries where these wonders are located. (See next page for answers.)

1. The Parthenon
2. The Giant's Causeway
3. The Suez Canal
4. The Vatican
5. Mount Everest
6. The Alps

7. The Pyramids
8. The Eiffel Tower

9. The Blarney Stone
10. The Hoover Dam
11. The Kremlin
12. The White Cliffs of Dover
13. The Great Wall

14. The Colosseum
15. The Leaning Tower
16. The Sahara
17. Table Mountain
18. Victoria Falls
19. The Golden Gate Bridge
20. The Taj Mahal

Answers: 1. Greece; 2. Northern Ireland; 3. Egypt; 4. Italy; 5. Tibet; 6. Mostly Switzerland; 7. Egypt; 8. France; 9. Ireland; 10. United States; 11. Russia; 12. England; 13. China; 14. Italy; 15. Italy; 16. North Africa; 17. South Africa; 18. Southern Rhodesia; 19. United States; 20. India.

Trip to the Moon. With youngsters as vividly interested in space exploration as they are, I always offer as first prize a trip to the moon to the winner of this true-and-false quiz.

1. The sun is the centre of the solar system.
2. The earth is a planet that revolves around the sun.
3. The sun is large enough to contain a million earths.
4. The sun is the largest of all stars.
5. The surface temperature of the sun is about 11,000° Fahrenheit.
6. The planets Pluto, Uranus, Mars, Saturn, Venus, Jupiter, Neptune, and Mercury can all be seen with the naked eye.
7. The sun never rotates.

8. It takes the earth one year to make its journey around the sun.
9. Mercury is the planet closest to the sun.
10. The earth is the only planet that has its own moon.
11. Scientists believe that Mars has an atmosphere.
12. The moon has an absolutely smooth surface.

Answers: 1. True; 2. True; 3. True; 4. False; 5. True; 6. False (you need a telescope to see Pluto, Uranus and Neptune); 7. False (it is constantly rotating slowly); 8. True; 9. True; 10. False (Jupiter has as many as twelve, and Saturn has nine. Others have fewer moons); 11. True; 12. False (it is broken up by many craters and mountain ridges).

History Quiz.

1. What was the Magna Carta and with what place in England is it associated?
2. On what date did the Mayflower sail from England? What was its purpose and where did it go?
3. What was the date of the Great Fire of London?
4. In what year was the Battle of Hastings fought?
5. What is meant by the "Declaration of Independence"?
6. Who were the Crusaders?
7. What were the weapons used during the Battle of Britain and who won it? What was the date?
8. Who were the first men to fly in a "heavier than air" machine and when was their maiden flight made?

9. Who made the first space flight around the earth and in what year?
10. In what century did Julius Caesar live?

Answers.

1. It was the "Great Charter" and has been described as "the Charter of English Liberties" which made law superior to the power of the king. It is associated with Runnymede (Surrey) where it was signed by King John in 1215.
2. The Mayflower sailed from England in 1620 carrying Puritans seeking religious freedom. They eventually landed at what is now Plymouth (Massachusetts, U.S.A.).
3. 1666
4. 1066
5. In 1776 the American Congress issued a Declaration of Independence stating that the United Colonies were free and independent states, severing all political association with Great Britain.
6. European princes and noblemen who set out during the 11th, 12th and 13th centuries on a series of crusades or religious wars to free Jerusalem from the Moslems.
7. Allied fighters (Spitfires and Hurricanes), German bombers and fighters and anti-aircraft guns. The battle was won by the Allied forces and was one of the main turning points of the Second World War. June–Oct, 1940.
8. The Wright brothers, Wilbur and Orville, in 1903.
9. Major Yuri Gagarin of the U.S.S.R. in 1961.
10. In the first century before Christ, from 102–44 B.C.

6

IT'S IN THE CARDS

MOST OF THE riddles, puzzles, and stunts you've read so far are good only until the moment the secret is out. Once, as I was travelling with the family and trying to wring another entertaining idea out of my head, I recalled with what patience and contentment the children often played cards at home. I wondered if it wouldn't be possible for them to play in the car. We tried it, and it works.

For a card table we lay a suitcase on its side on the back seat, and cover the suitcase with a cloth to keep the cards from sliding about. When the three children play, Susan sits in the middle, with the suitcase on her lap, while the two smaller children sit sideways on either side of her.

Where the game does not call for many cards spread out on the table, the children can sit and up-end a large suitcase in front of them.

We reserve card-playing for smooth roads, but there are plenty of those on the average trip.

An adult who is not driving will have to teach some of these games. Others, the children already know. Card games do have some merits for children. I think it improves their sense of numbers and helps them develop logical thinking habits and careful observation.

These games also help children to learn to win or lose with grace. Sometimes Pam or I join in these games, and the children enjoy this because they are competing with us on fairly equal terms. As in most children's card games, the element of luck is a little stronger than the element of skill.

Slap Jack. For two or three children. Place a shuffled pack face down on the suitcase. Each player in turn takes a card from the top of the pack and places it face up on the "face-up" pile. Whenever a Jack shows, all the players must clap hands overhead *twice*, and then try to slap the Jack. The child who first slaps the Jack wins it and all the cards underneath it in the "face-up" pile. These cards are placed in the child's *own* pile. This goes on until the Jacks have been exposed and captured. The child who slaps the last Jack also wins whatever cards remain in the "face-down" pile.

When the cards are used up, players count their piles and write their scores on a sheet of paper. The child who has the highest score after the game has been repeated three or four times is the winner.

War for Two. Two players. Deal twenty-six cards to each player. Players turn the cards face down in front of them. At a signal, each child turns up his top card. The child who has the higher of these two cards collects them both and puts them under his own stack. (In this game the King is high and the Ace is low.)

If the two cards turned up are the same (two fives, Queens, etc.) there is "war". Each player turns one card face down and then a second card face-up. The higher of the two new face-up cards wins the war and its owner takes all six cards. If the second face-up cards are also the same, there is a "double-war". The process is repeated, and this time the winner takes all ten cards.

The game goes on like this until one player has all the cards. Paradoxically, I've seen it help and keep peace among the children for as much as sixty miles.

War for Three. This is the same as the previous game, but adapted to three players. Remove one card from the pack and then deal seventeen cards to each player. At the signal, the three players turn up their top cards and the winner takes all. If all three cards turned up match, there is "war for three". If only two of them match, but they are topped by the third card, the player who uncovered that card would win. But if the two matching cards are higher than the third card, only the two who uncovered matching cards would have a "war", and the other player would be out of it—although his card would be lost.

Pig. Three players can play this lively game, but it's much better with four or even five.

Prepare a pack with four cards of a kind for each player in the game. For instance, for three players the pack would have twelve cards: four Aces, four Kings, four Queens. If there are four players, add four Jacks and so on.

The dealer shuffles and deals four cards to each player. The purpose of the game is either to get four of a kind in your own hand or to notice it when someone else does. Each player looks at his hand to see if he has four of a kind. If no one has, each player puts an unneeded card (one that is not in a pair) face down on the suitcase and passes it to his left. At the same time he receives a card from the player on his right. He puts this card in his hand to see if it makes four of a kind. If no one has four of a kind, the players again pass a card face down to the left.

The game continues until one player gets four of a kind. That player immediately stops passing and places his forefinger on his nose. The other children must see this, stop passing, and place *their* fingers on their noses. The last child to wake up is the "Pig".

In this game it is as important for the player to be alert and watch the other players as it is to play his own hand.

Old Maid. This is an old favourite involving three, four, or five players. Remove three Queens from a pack. The remaining Queen is the Old Maid. Deal the cards, one at a time, until they are all gone. Each player then examines his hand and discards all pairs by placing them face up on the suitcase. After all pairs have been discarded, play begins.

The first player offers his hand (with the card faces hidden) to the player on his left. The second player selects one card, takes it, and puts it in his own hand. If it makes a pair, he discards as before. He then offers his hand to the player on *his* left, who makes a selection.

This continues until more and more pairs are discarded. Since there is no other Queen for the Old Maid to pair with, she will be the last card left. The player stuck with the Old Maid at the end of the game is the loser.

Fish. Two to five players. When two or three play, deal seven cards to each player. When four or five play, deal five cards each. Place all remaining cards in a face-down pack.

The purpose of the game is to form as many "sets" (four of a kind) as possible.

Pamela begins by asking, "Have you any threes, Susan?" If she has, she *must* give them to her mother, who puts them in her hand. Pam then has a turn to ask again, and she may ask *any* player for *any* card. However, if Susan has no threes, she tells Pam to "fish". Pam then draws a card from the pack. If the card is what she asked for, she shows it to the others, keeps it, and has another turn at asking for a card. If it is *not* what she asked for, the player on her left now has a turn to ask for a card.

Whenever a player gets four of a kind, he places this "set" on the table in front of him where the others can see it. Then he has another turn. If a player is left without cards when his turn comes, he draws a card from the pack and then asks another player for a card of that valve. When the pack has been used up, a player without cards is out of the game.

When all thirteen "sets" have been collected and placed on the table, the player with the most "sets" wins.

Concentration. For two or three children, preferably six or older. It takes your biggest suitcase.

Shuffle a pack of cards and distribute them face down at random on whatever surface you are using. Each player in turn picks up two cards, and leaves them face up where they are. If the two cards make a pair, he takes them and places them face down in his own pile. If they do not make a pair, he turns them over again in the same spot in which he turned them up.

The game continues. Each player tries to pick up a pair when his turn comes. The trick is to remember where previous cards have been shown and then turned over again. Thus, if a player turns up a Jack and remembers where another Jack was previously uncovered he can make a pair. Picking up a pair gives the player another turn. The player with the most cards in his stack wins.

Seven of a Kind. Three, four, or five players. If there are three players, prepare a pack of twenty-one cards, with seven cards in each of three suits. If there are four players prepare a pack of twenty-eight cards, seven in each of four suits. For five players, make it thirty-five in the pack with eight or nine in each suit.

Shuffle thoroughly and deal seven cards to each player. The purpose of the game is to get seven cards of the same suit in your hand. Each player looks at his hand and passes an unwanted card to his left, as in "Pig". The idea is to keep cards that give promise of building into a strong suit, and unload isolated cards. The first player to hold seven of a kind may call out, "Seven of a kind!", or he may put his finger to his nose as in "Pig".

As play continues, you may find that another player is apparently saving the same suit as you, since none of these cards is coming your way. When this happens, you may have to break up your suit and start again.

Go Boom. Two or more players.

Deal seven cards to each player. Place the remaining cards face down in a pack. The first player starts by putting any card on the suitcase, face up. The player on his left must then play a card that matches it either in value or suit. For instance, if the first card played is the five of Clubs, the next player can put down any Club, or any other five. If he put down the nine of Clubs, the *next* player would have to match that, by playing either any nine or any Club. So it goes, as each player takes his turn at playing a matching card. Whenever a player cannot match the previous card, he must draw from the pack until he *is* able to play. If a player uses up the pack without finding a card that is playable, he says "pass", and the next player has a turn.

The game goes on until one player gets rid of all his cards. He is the winner.

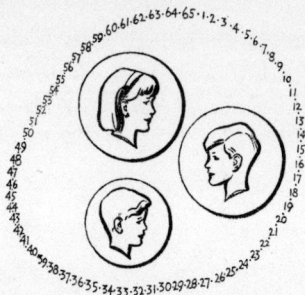

7

NUMERALS AND COINS

D O YOU WANT to tell a person's age, discover a Magic Square, put together eight 8s to make 1,000, or locate a mysterious number that someone else has in mind? These are a few of the things children can do with coin puzzles and mathematical teasers.

Most of these puzzles depend on logic and imagination rather than advanced mathematics. The solutions are not "trick" solutions, but legitimate answers to legitimate problems.

MATHEMATICAL TEASERS

Doing It the Hard Way. How can you write a number that is equivalent to 100 by using six 9s?

Solution: $$99 + \frac{99}{99}$$

77

Eight 8s? How can you write a number that is equivalent to 1,000 by using eight 8s?

Solution:
$$8$$
$$8$$
$$8$$
$$88$$
$$+888$$
____

Fresh Herrings. If a herring and a half cost three-halfpence and the herring cost 1d more than the half, how much did the herring cost?

Solution: The herring cost $1\frac{1}{4}$d and the half cost $\frac{1}{4}$d.

The Price of Oranges. The grocer, feeling generous on his birthday, said to his assistant, "Change the price of oranges so that they'll be sold at a shilling a dozen less than the present price. That means that customers will get one more orange for each shilling." What were the old and new prices of the oranges?

Solution: The old price was three for a shilling. The new price is four for a shilling.

Strange Subtraction. Take 1 from 19 and get 20—if you can.

Solution: You can do it if you use Roman numerals. From XIX, take I and you get XX. (This, of course, is a trick and not a legitimate mathematical problem.)

Silly 7s. Can you arrange three 7s so that they will equal 20?

Solution: $7 + 7 \div .7$

78

Growing Older. The sum of our ages is twenty-two. I will be seven times as old as you are now when I become twice your present age. How old am I? (You can solve this one by algebra or by good old trial-and-error.)

Solution: I am eighteen. This means that you are now four. Ten years from now I will be twenty-eight, and you will be fourteen, so I'll be twice your age. And twenty-eight is seven times as old as four.

PUZZLES AND TRICKS WITH NUMBERS

You can solve some of the following puzzles by really knitting your brows and going to work. Others are based on good-natured fraud.

Magic Square. Give the players a sheet of paper and a pencil. Ask them to draw a large square and

2	9	4
7	5	3
6	1	8

divide it into nine smaller boxes. Tell them they are to fill in the nine boxes with the numbers 1 to 9, placing one number in each box. But the total in every row, whether vertical, horizontal, or diagonal, must add up to fifteen.

The diagram shows one solution. It's important to have 5 in the centre box; then the outer diagonal numbers, and the centre outer numbers horizontally and vertically must add up to ten.

Nineteen Yaks. A dying Tibetan chieftain called his three sons together to tell them he was leaving them his herd of yaks. The oldest son would get half the herd, the second son would get one quarter, and the youngest one fifth. When the chieftain died the sons started to divide the herd, but they found there were 19 yaks. Since they could not divide 19 by 2, 4, or 5, they appealed to a neighbouring wise man. He divided the herd so they were all satisfied. How did he do it?

Solution: The wise man temporarily added one of his own yaks to the herd, making twenty. He then divided them, giving half (10) to the oldest son, a quarter (5) to the next, and a fifth (4) to the last son. This left one over, which he took back, and everybody was happy.

Correct Age. This stunt makes you appear to be a genius. If you're mean you can hang on to this reputation and refuse to explain the trick. You can tell anyone's age by what appears to be mysterious mathematics. Ask any person to think of his exact age, but not to tell you. (If you are playing with a child who knows you are aware of his age, you can simply ask him to think of any number and you will tell him what it is.) Now tell the person you are playing with to multiply his age (or his number) by 3, then add 6, and then divide by 3.

You ask for the result. Mentally, you subtract 2 from the answer. This gives you the person's correct age, or the number he was thinking of.

Solution: Let's say you played with a boy aged ten. He multiplies by 3 and gets 30. He adds 6 and gets 36. He divides by 3 and gets 12, and he announces this result. You subtract 2, and you have it. It works with any number.

Magic Numbers. Games of this type are always attractive to children who can carry out simple calculations. If children can't manage them in their heads, let them have pencil and paper.

Ask a player to think of any number. He picks:	8
Double it	16
Add 4	20
Multiply by 5	100
Add 12	112
Multiply by 10	1120

At this point you ask him to give you the number he has reached. He will, of course, say 1120. No matter what the number is, you subtract 320. This gives you 800. Now strike out the last two noughts and this gives you 8. Announce that his original number was 8, and you will be right.

More Magic Numbers. Although this deals with smaller figures it's even a little trickier. Children will have to use paper and pencil for this one unless they are little geniuses.

1. Ask a person to think of a number. He chooses: 9

2. Ask him to multiply it by itself.   81
3. Ask him to subtract 1 from the original numbers 8
4. Ask him to multiply this number by itself.   64
5. Ask him to subtract this number (step 4) from the
   first product (step 2), and tell you the difference.
   You then add 1 to this number, getting 18, and
   divide it in half, which gives you 9, the original
   number.

How many Pennies? There's no real trick to this,
but it helps children understand how easy it is to be
far off in a visual estimate. Ask them how many
pennies lying flat and piled one on top of the
other would be needed to reach the same height as a
penny standing on its edge. Almost all children
will underestimate the number. (So will almost all
adults.) The usual guess is six or eight flat pennies.
The answer is a minimum of 12, depending on how
worn they are.

Odd and Even. This is a mysterious stunt like
"Magic Numbers". Ask any child in the car to
hold an odd number of coins in one hand and an
even number in the other. Only he knows which is
which, but you will tell him which hand is odd and
which is even if he performs a simple mathematical
calculation for you.

Ask him to multiply the coins in his right hand by
two (or any even number he chooses), and those in
his left hand by three (or any odd number). Now
let him add the two resulting numbers and tell you
the total.

You will know that if this total is odd, the number of coins in the right hand is even and that in the left hand is odd. If the total he gives you is even, the reverse is true.

The bright ones will be able to work out the trick, and it's simply this: If you multiply an odd number by another odd number, the result is odd, while if you multiply an even by an odd number, the result is even.

Seven Coins. In the diagram below are seven coins. Place coins on a sheet of paper just as in the diagram. Now put each coin into a separate space or compartment by drawing straight lines across the square. But you are allowed only three straight lines to do the job.

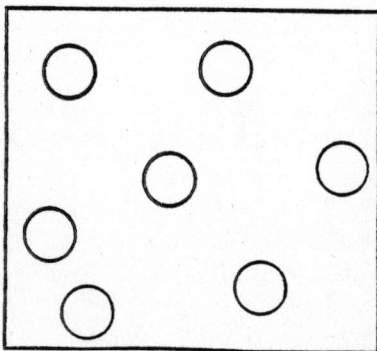

Give up? See illustration on the next page.

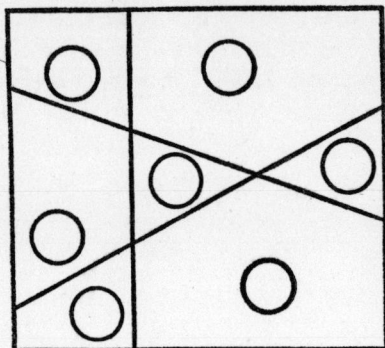

Coin Teaser. Arrange six coins in the form of a cross. Now move just one coin and have two rows of four coins each.

Solution: Place the lowest coin on top of the centre one, slightly overlapping it, as shown.

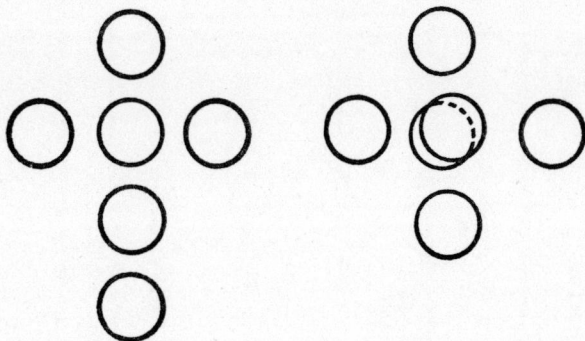

Jumping Coins. Draw a square and divide it into twenty-five smaller boxes as in the following illustration. Put coins, or small pieces of paper marked with the numbers 1 to 9 in the boxes, as shown.

The problem is to get rid of all the coins but one by jumping as in draughts. You may jump across, up, down, or diagonally. Whenever you jump over a coin, remove it from the board. But what makes this puzzle tough is that the final coin *must* be left in the centre square.

Solution: Take 9 and jump over 4, 5, 7, and 1. Then have 3 jump over 2. Then take 6 and jump over 8 and 3. End by jumping 9 over 6. Nine will be the only coin remaining and it will be in the centre square.

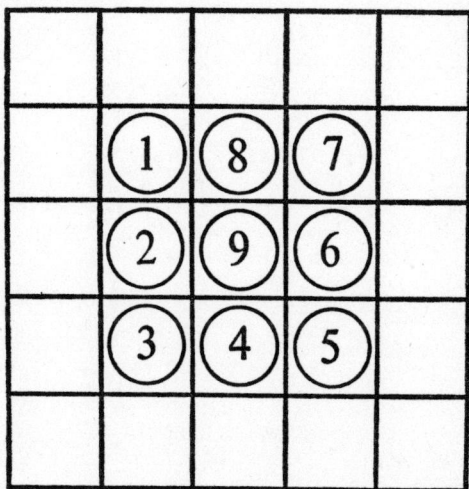

More Jumping Coins. Lay three pennies and three sixpences in a row, as shown. Now make three moves, moving two adjacent coins at a time. You must wind up so that every other coin in the line is different (they alternate in value). You must not leave any open spaces between coins at the end.

Solution: Move coins 1 and 2 to the right of coin 6. Move coins 6 and 1 to the right of 2. Move coins 3 and 4 to the right of 5. That does it!

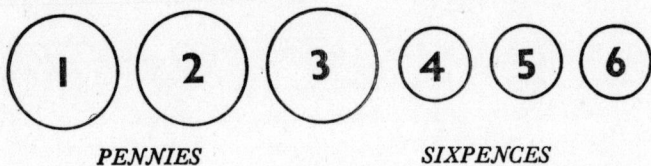

PENNIES   *SIXPENCES*

8

NOVELTY DRAUGHTS
AND PUZZLES

SUSAN AND MICHAEL play draughts, and David is just learning. It's a good game for car travel since it takes a fairly long time to play. There are various sorts of draught-boards made especially for travelling.

If regular draughts begin to lose appeal for the children, we have a number of variations on the game.

Give-away Draughts. This is regular draughts in reverse. The object is to be the first to *lose* all your draughts, and it's not easy when the other player is trying to do the same thing. It takes as much strategy as in ordinary draughts to move your men so that they must be taken, and to avoid having to jump your rival's draughts. Jumps *must* be taken, although if two or more different jumps are available at the same time, you can choose the least damaging one.

Hunter and Wolves. This is a "chase" game played with four draughts. The "hunter", a white draught, is in a corner square. The "wolves", three black draughts, are in the opposite corner, guarding the "cabin". The player who controls the hunter tries to get him safely through the wolves and into the cabin. The player who controls the wolves tries to capture the hunter by jumping him. When a wolf is jumped it is removed from the board. In this game moves may be made in any direction *except the diagonal*.

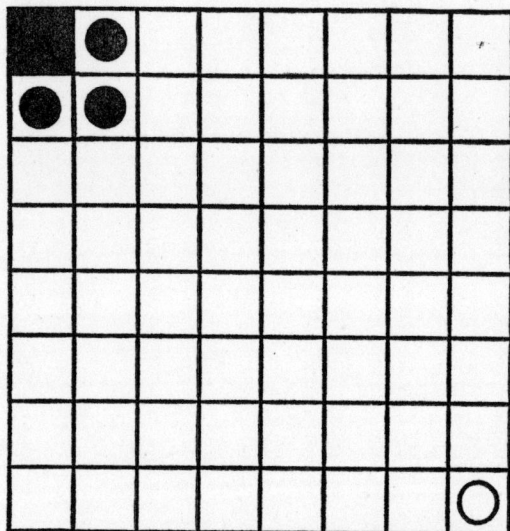

Draughts and Crosses. This is a form of Noughts and Crosses played with draughts. One player has five black men; the other five white ones. They take turns setting their draughts down in the boxes on a regular draught-board. The purpose of the game is to get five draughts in a row, vertically, horizontally, or diagonally. If no one has five draughts in a row when all ten draughts are down, the play continues. The players take turns moving one square at a time in any direction (no jumping) until someone wins.

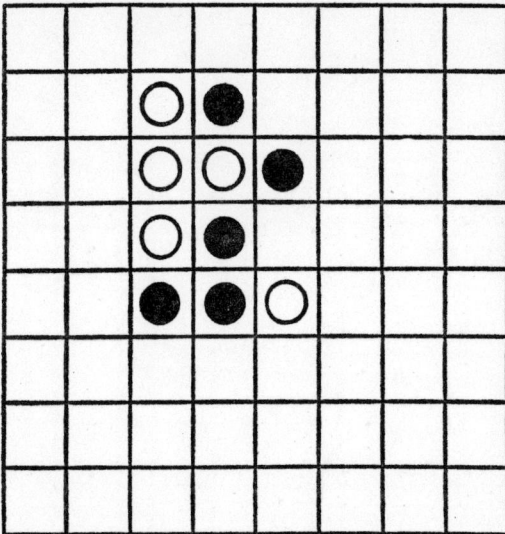

Six-Man Football. Two players compete, one with six black and the other with six white draughts. Put a drawing-pin in one draught to represent the "football". The player who has the "football" tries to move it across the field into the last row on his opponent's side of the ball.

Move the draughts one square at a time in any direction *except the diagonal*. When a draught is jumped it is *not* removed from the board. Possession of the "football" changes on the following basis: when a player jumps the "football", he removes the drawing-pin and places it on the draught that did the jumping. Now he is in possession and he tries to move it towards his opponent's goal line.

The first player to score three goals wins, or you can set a time limit.

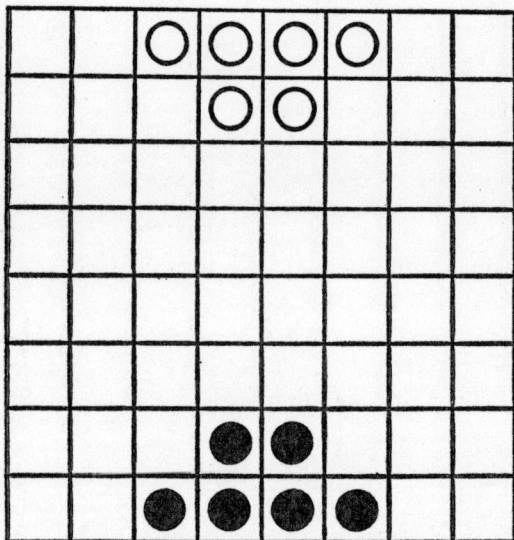

DRAUGHT-BOARD PUZZLES

One in a Line. Take eight draughts and try to place them on the draught-board so that no more than one draught is in any one line, vertically, horizontally, or diagonally. It's a rare child who can solve this in under thirty minutes. He'll probably give up after fifteen, and you'll have to show him.

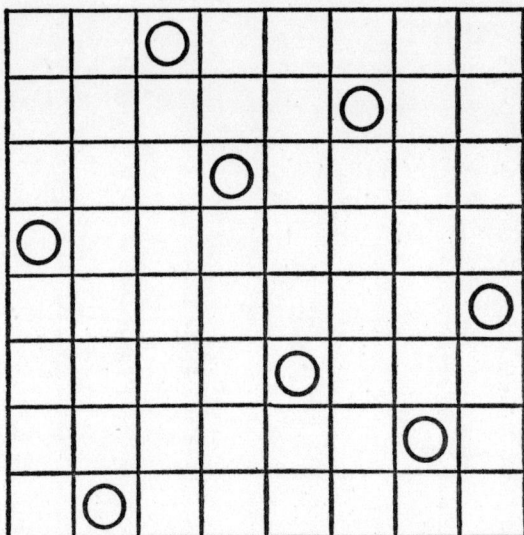

Right and Left. This is a tricky one. Draw a row of seven boxes on a piece of paper. Place three white draughts in the boxes on the left, and three black draughts in the boxes on the right.

The trick is to transfer the draughts so that the white ones will be on the right and the black ones on the left. The black ones may move *only* to the left, the white ones *only* to the right. Move each draught one box at a time unless jumping. Single jumps are permitted. The transfer must be completed in exactly fifteen moves.

Solution: Obey these two simple rules.

1. Start with a draught of either colour and move it. After every *single* move by a draught of one colour, make a jump with the other colour.

2. After each jump, advance with the same colour that made the jump. The position of the draughts will show whether you should make another jump or just a single move.

After the ninth move these rules no longer apply, but the remaining moves should be obvious. Fifteen moves will do the trick.

Two in a Line. This is even tougher than the previous puzzles. Take sixteen draughts and try to place them on the board so that only two—no more—are in each line, vertically, horizontally and diagonally.

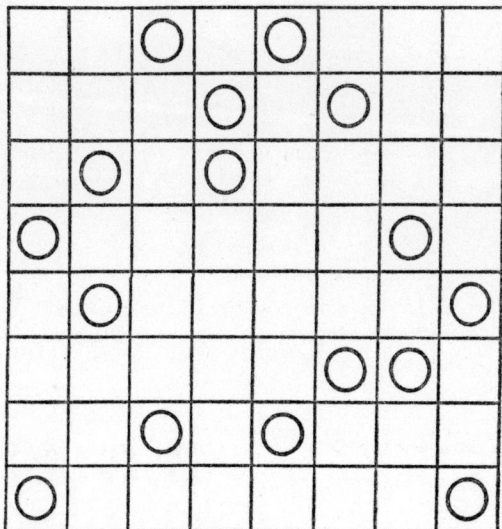

9

DRAWING GAMES AND SIMPLE CRAFTS

Mₒₛₜ CHILDREN LIKE to draw. A car is no place for wet paints, scissors or sharp pencils, but soft crayons, pencils and a supply of paper do well enough.

We give our children clip-boards to work on. You can also use a drawing-board, a stiff-cover book, or the side of a suitcase.

Sometimes we just set the children up and let them doodle and draw as their fancy dictates. At other times we suggest ideas, or propose one of the following games:

DRAWING GAMES

Doodles. Pamela draws a few on a sheet of paper. They may be straight, spiralling or curved lines.

Anything that comes into her head will do. Then she hands the doodles to the children, whose job it is to incorporate them into a picture. An example:

The doodles should have few lines and remain simple or it will be too hard for the child to incorporate them into a drawing that makes sense. Sometimes the children play this among themselves, but they also like to challenge us to complete doodles that they prepare.

Initials. This is similar to "Doodles", but here the challenge is to let the child draw his initials and then incorporate them into a picture. For instance, Thomas Marlowe's initials are T. M.:

Pebble Pictures. Take several pebbles and let them drop at random on a sheet of paper. The child draws a dot wherever a pebble lands. Then he must create a picture that includes all these dots.

Blind Elephants. Give a child paper and pencil, blindfold him, and ask him to draw an elephant. The results are usually amusing. Sometimes we add the rule that the pencil may not be lifted from the paper at any time, except to draw the eye and the tail. These probably wind up totally detached from the elephant's body. This can also be a contest to see which child draws the best "blind elephant".

House in a Fog. This is another blindfold game. The blindfolded child is told to draw a house, step by step. The child, however, does not draw on his own. We tell him every item we want him to draw—the roof, the side walls, the chimney, the front door, etc. (Michael was once annoyed because we left off the TV aerial.) Remove the blindfold when the picture is finished. It seldom bears any resemblance to a house.

Map of Home. This little game is good for helping children achieve a sense of space. Ask them to draw a map of home. Little children might try just the house, the garden, and the street, or, in the case of a city child, the layout of the flat. Older children might try their hand at a real map of their community, showing the school, the post-office, various roads, the homes of friends, and other landmarks.

You might also try letting the children collaborate on a joint project, using as large a sheet of paper as possible, colouring the drawing in full, and indicating an approximate scale of distance and points of the compass.

Curiously enough, this game is reassuring to small children who get a little homesick on a long trip.

You Name It. This game needs someone with a knack for drawing to get it started. The idea is to draw an animal whose ancestors were fast and loose. As a result of misconduct on the part of his progenitors, the animal has: (1) The head of an elephant; (2) the antlers of a moose; (3) the stripes of a tiger; (4) the tail of a beaver; (5) the front legs of a horse; (6) and the hindquarters of a kangaroo. Make up your own combinations as you go along.

After you draw this beast, let the children guess the various animals from which it is descended. Then they can try drawing their own composite animals, letting each other guess the lineage.

HANDWORK GAMES

Handicrafts for children in a car have to be limited to materials that are safe. But there's plenty to do within these limitations. We find that our children like clay or plasticine modelling, simple plaiting and raffia work, and various cut-and-paste projects. (For cutting we give them nursing scissors with blunt ends.) If you're a station-wagon family and can set aside a space at the back for this sort of thing, it's a great help.

Before we take a trip, I usually stop at a hobby shop, an arts-and-crafts shop, or the educational games section of a department store. I browse around and pick up any number of materials to take along.

Thirty Links. This is a contest for two children. Give each of them several sheets of coloured paper, scissors, and a box of paper clips. At a signal each child starts to cut out thirty coloured strips of paper. Then he makes links of them, and attaches each link to the next with a paper clip, making a chain of links. The first child to complete thirty links is the winner.

Four children can play this in teams of two each. Each team works on its own chain (from opposite ends). After five miles, the game is stopped and the team with the most links wins. Part of the fun of the game is in keeping the links from coming apart, since they are held together only by paper clips.

Picture Paste-up. Before leaving on a trip, collect several good magazines that have colourful pictures of people, places, and things.

Then, when you're on the road and the children fall into that lull that precedes the storm, give them each several magazines, scissors, a tube of paste, a box of crayons, and a large stiff sheet of paper. Now ask them to cut out a variety of pictures—people, animals, cars, houses, birds, whatever catches their fancy. Then ask them to paste their picture clippings on the large sheets, each child making a single picture that makes some sense (more or less). The children can use the crayons to fill in additional details or background. You'll find that the children will come up with some colourful and pleasing montages.

Home-made Jigsaw Puzzles. Each child cuts out a single large colourful picture from a magazine and mounts it with paste or rubber cement on a sheet of cardboard. Then the child draws a number of curving lines on the back, dividing the sheet into many small sections. At the next stop or picnic, an adult can cut the picture into sections with a pen-knife or razor blade in a holder. The child now has a jigsaw puzzle that he has made himself, and other members of the family can do the puzzle.

Alphabet Book. Hang on to your picture magazines because we're going to use them again. Equip each child with a fairly large hard-cover notebook. Then let them work singly or as a team on one "Alphabet Book". Their first job is to cut out large capital letters from the magazine and paste them in alphabetical order in the upper left-hand corner of successive pages of the notebook.

Now they must cut out a variety of pictures from the magazines and paste them in the notebook under the proper letter. Thus cars, clowns, and cabbages will go on Page C. Lions, lace, lutes, and lawns go on Page L. The goal is to fill the entire book, including Page X.

This will take quite a while, but don't let that bother you. It's the kind of game that children put aside for a time and return to later. And it's excellent spelling practice for youngsters who are just starting on the three Rs.

Pipe-cleaner Sculpture. Give a child a handful of pipe-cleaners and tell him he's Henry Moore. Imaginative youngsters work these fluffy, pliable cleaners into animals, birds, people, planes and mechanical objects.

(Some shops sell brightly coloured pipe-cleaners. These are the best.)

Crayon Leaf Prints. Instead of just copying or tracing the outlines of leaves, children will get more impressive results with crayon leaf prints.

Place a green live leaf on a flat smooth surface. Put a sheet of white paper over it. The child now rubs the paper gently and steadily with a crayon, holding it lightly with one hand so the leaf will not move. As the child does this, the edges, veins, and stem of the leaf will gradually appear, creating a delicate and attractive picture. A child can also place several leaves with interesting outlines on a single sheet in an attractive pattern. By using

different-coloured crayons for each leaf, he will
create an unusual effect.

Paper-bag Puppets. Keep all the white paper bags
that come your way. Let the children draw facial
features on the bags with crayon. Now they have
"puppets", put a "puppet" over each child's
hand and tie it at the wrist with string or an elastic
band. And then, probably without invitation, the
children will tell stories or act out playlets, using
the puppet characters as actors.

You can also use old woollen stockings in the
same way. If you have odd scraps of coloured
material and knitting wool, these will do to make
the features. Older children can sew these on with
their mother's help.

Paper bags also make simple face masks. Cut
out slits for the eyes and mouth, and draw the other
features with crayon. Let the children put these
over their heads and use them for informal dramatic
fun, just as they do with puppets. (And don't worry.
Paper bags are perfectly safe. It's the plastic bags
you must keep out of their hands.)

10

STUNTS AND TRICKS

THE STUNTS AND tricks that follow are mostly physical. They involve either finger-play or the use of such props as handkerchiefs, string or blunt scissors. I have also included a few simple "mental telepathy" tricks.

Now most children, especially the younger ones, will not be able to solve these puzzles. But that doesn't matter. The puzzles will intrigue them, and they will get their pleasure when they finally discover the secret of each trick. Then they will practise it themselves.

FINGER PLAYS

"*Tommy, Tommy.*" Point with the index finger of your left hand to the little finger of your right hand, and then to each finger in turn, saying these words, "Tommy, Tommy, Tommy, Tommy, Whoops, Tommy."

You say "Whoops" as you slide down the index finger of the right hand then up the thumb. Repeat the action in the opposite direction, starting with the thumb, and saying, "Tommy, Whoops, Tommy, Tommy, Tommy, Tommy." Then fold your arms quietly and challenge any child to repeat what you have done. The point is that after doing the finger-play and saying the words exactly, they must *fold their arms* as you have done.

Only a very alert child will catch on at once and fold his arms. Do it again, and make the arm-folding a little more obvious, then let the children have another try at it. Sooner or later one child will detect the secret.

As an added variation you can clear your throat loudly before doing the "Tommy, Tommy" pattern. Children must detect and imitate this as well.

Eleven Fingers. Pam begins by saying to Michael, "I have eleven fingers, counting my thumbs, and I can prove it!"

Using her right index finger, she touches each finger of her left hand, counting, "One, two, three, four, five." Then she touches the fingers of her right hand with her left index finger, counting, "Six, seven, eight, nine, ten." (Michael thinks this is really a great joke. How can his mother be so backward?)

"That's queer," says Pam. "I was *sure* I had eleven fingers. Let me count them again."

Now she counts backwards, pointing to the fingers of her left hand, "Ten, nine, eight, seven, six." Then she quickly holds up her right hand and says, "And five are eleven!"

The Semi-detached Thumb. This stunt makes it appear as if you are pulling you thumb apart and then making it whole again, without surgery.

Hold your left hand forward, palm facing you, and fingers extended. Bend the left thumb at the joint so that half of it is hidden to the observer. Then bend your right thumb and place it along the index finger of the left hand so that it looks like an extension of the left thumb. Cover the joint with your right index finger.

Slowly move the right thumb down the left index finger. Close your eyes as if in pain and groan. It looks as if you're pulling the left thumb apart. Then slowly return the right hand to the starting position.

The illusion will impress young children (although with no sense of horror whatsoever). Older children will think you're rather silly, but they'll want to learn the trick themselves anyway.

MENTAL TELEPATHY

All these little stunts should be done by one adult in league with a child, or by an older child and a younger one. They have to be prepared in advance so that the magician and his assistant get their signals straight. Usually the assistant "reads" the magician's mind while the magician squints his eyes and concentrates fiercely in the effort to telepathize.

Black Magic. This was the speciality of Susan and Michael. Susan is blindfolded. The others in the car pick a secret object. We take the blindfold off Susan. Michael then points to a series of objects without saying a word. When he points to the right one, Susan immediately identifies it.

Solution: Susan and Michael have agreed that Michael will point to something coloured black just before he points at the correct object. This gives Susan her clue. Now and then they change the tip-off colour.

Not That One. Play this exactly as above, except that now the accomplice rather than the magician gives the tip-off. After the blindfold is off the accomplice, the magician points to a series of objects. The accomplice shakes his head or says "No". Eventually the accomplice says, "Not that one". The phrase, "not that one", is the signal for the magician to point at the correct object next.

Secret House. Michael is in league with his mother. Michael covers his ears and closes his eyes. The rest of us pick a secret hour of day. Pam then asks him to guess the chosen hour, and he never fails.

Solution: The first letter of the first word that Pam says to Michael is the tip-off. If she says, "Don't make a mistake now, Michael," he knows that the secret hour is four, because D is the fourth letter of the alphabet. If Pam begins with, "Hope you can guess this, Michael," H is the eighth letter, and the hour is eight o'clock.

It takes a little time for Pam and Michael to

work out their signals each time, but you just can't hurry mental telepathy.

Magic Date. While letting my wife drive for a while, I declare that I can read the date on a coin through a piece of opaque paper, without lifting the paper or looking under it. Then, stipulating only that the coin be fairly new and that it must lie reverse up, I let Susan put it on a book or suitcase and cover it with a sheet of paper.

I take a pencil and rub it lightly over the paper directly on top of the coin. Gradually an impression of the coin shows through until I am able to read the date. (It won't work with a small or worn coin.)

II

CAR FUN FOR YOUNGER
CHILDREN

S O FAR WE'VE played games that are appropriate
for youngsters between the ages of five and fourteen. But what about the three- four- or five-year-
old?

He can't read or write, so word games don't mean
much to him. He can probably count to ten, but he
doesn't understand numbers well enough to solve
arithmetical problems or do counting games.

However, many of the suggestions in this book are
good for younger children if you all have the patience
to play them simply and slowly, and it is worth while
to make a special effort to provide special kinds of
free, expressive, individual and group play that will be
just right for very young children.

USING GAMES IN "FUN ON WHEELS"

Let's try to adapt some of the simpler activities in this book for the three- to five-year-old child. Suppose we begin with road signs. Older children learn to read and recognize them. The youngsters can learn certain things. Even the child who cannot yet read letters can recognize some signs by their special shapes or colours. When the red light appears, it will be a four-year-old who can say "Stop!" or who can call "That's a train crossing" when he spots a level-crossing sign.

In a game like Continued Story (page 28), where each player picks up the thread of a narrative and carries it along, the pre-school child can certainly take part. His story will be simpler, but within the realms of his own experience he is making as big a contribution as anyone.

Here are some of the games you can adapt for younger passengers.

In chapter 1, the young child can join in Guess What I Saw (page 16) and I Hear (page 23) as well as other observation games. In Highway Observation (page 15) an older brother or sister should tell him a few specific things to look for—a pond, a motor-cycle policeman, a bridge. When he spots one of these, shower him with praise. That keeps him happy, too.

In Chapter 2, even three-year-olds can take part in simple physical stunts such as Opposites (page 34), Fingers and Fists (page 35), Make 'em Laugh (page 34), and Rub and Pat (page 34). Do this and Add Something (page 31) is a possibility. Some young children can play guessing games like Shopping on Account (page 26) and I'm Thinking of a Word (page 26). It's important for the older children to be patient with them and give them a hand.

Word games in Chapter 3 and the quizzes in Chapter 4 are too difficult for children below the age of seven or eight, but they can help to recognize pictures in Scrambled Animals (page 40), and parents can make up special quizzes for them at their own level. Simple questions on familiar subjects are what is wanted, like

"Who puts bottles outside our door every morning?" (The milkman)
"Which animal does milk come from?" (The cow)
"Which goes faster, a car or a bicycle?" (A car)
"Which is hotter, the sun or the moon?" (The sun)
"One of these animals lives in the water: the lion, the horse, the whale. Which one?" (The whale)

Make these little quizzes seem part of everyone's game. Play a more difficult quiz with the older children, and then say, "Now we'll have a special one for Peter. Everybody else be quiet and see if he can answer." He will be delighted with his special quiz—and the special attention he is getting.

All children will like the material in Chapter 4, Chestnuts Old and New. The meaning of the more subtle riddles may escape the very young child, but most of them will amuse him. Remember what an appreciative audience you have in him. No matter how old and corny the riddles are, he is probably hearing them for the first time in his life.

Puzzles like Rock in the Cellar (page 48) or Low Bridge (page 49), which are not too technical, will interest him even though he cannot answer them himself. Noughts and Crosses (page 52) and some of the "challenges" will also amuse him.

I've learned the trick of involving pre-school children in simple card games and draughts contests. It may be hard for a child that young to understand the rules. I make an attempt to explain and then I simply go ahead and play the game. Once we start, I'm not too particular about enforcing the rules of play. Sometimes I suspend the rules and let the youngster play as he imagines he should. I find that with this approach, a pre-school child picks up the fundamentals of a simple game very quickly and soon has a grasp of the rules.

As you know, the young child has to win fairly often. You must carry him when he's learning a game. If you beat him promptly and regularly, he'll only get frustrated, throw the board out of the window and kick the door. Understanding older brothers and sisters may take delight in the ingenuity needed to lose to a youngster. When he really plays the game properly, he will be more ready to lose now and then.

With this approach, young children can gradually learn simple games like Slap Jack (page 71), War for Two (page 72) and even Concentration (page 75).

Some five-year-olds can play novelty draught games like Hunter and Wolves (page 88).

Be patient. The five-year-old will be confused at first, but when he grasps the simple rules of play, the game will be fun for him.

The drawing games in Chapter 9 are probably too confining for very young children. They like to draw freely. But it doesn't hurt to try them out. Four- and five-year-olds can handle the cutting and pasting games in this chapter.

Youngsters will not be able to perform the illusions and tricks in Chapter 10, but they will enjoy watching others do them.

FREE PLAY ACTIVITIES

Most young children are very talented at keeping themselves occupied once they have the toys and materials handy to spark their imaginations. A thoughtful parent can make a list of the play equipment his child is most fond of, things that are practical in a car. It always helps to add some surprise items for good measure, and a cardboard box with the child's name on it is indispensable.

This might hold:

Dolls and doll clothing, doll's bed, doctor or nurse set, play cooking utensils and dishes, play telephone.

Nests of hollow blocks or cubes, small construction sets, wooden cars, trucks, planes.

Coloured paper, crayons, modelling clay, blunt scissors, cut-up magazines, paste, sticky tape.

Cast-off clothing, hats, scarves, old handbags (for play-acting).

Then, if this material sparks off the child's imagination, play *with* him, being careful not to dominate or to turn the direction of play needlessly.

Mechanical gadgets and toys that give a child little more than the chance to press a button or turn a lever are not worth the space they take up. The best equipment is that which a youngster can manipulate and use expressively. It's best to avoid breakable objects and things so small that they are easily lost.

At the end of each day's travel, all the child's play material should go back into the cardboard box.

MUSICAL FUN

Find space for a few simple musical instruments or toys—a little drum, a tambourine, cymbals or a triangle, a toy xylophone or anything which children can use to tap out a rhythm. True, these things make a noise, but a good musical or mechanical sound is preferable to the determined whining of an impatient, restless child.

The mysteries of rhythm intrigue children. They like to discover the beat in things. Let them use the instruments in as many ways as possible, experimenting with the different sounds, accompanying singing, exploring metres or tempos. Encourage them to imitate the rhythm of animals, trains and planes. What is the music of a horse trotting? What is the music of a train coming into a station? Ask them to play sentences musically, without the use of words—preferably lines from heavily accented rhymes.

Try teaching songs to little children. In addition to the familiar songs, they delight in making up new ones. Use familiar tunes like " Pop Goes the Weasel " or "Here We Go Round the Mulberry Bush", and let the four-year-old invent songs about the trip, the family, friends, nursery school, fire engines—the whole wide world.

This kind of improvised music is akin to story-telling. Children love stories and if you run out of new ones, they always have a few old favourites they like to hear over and over again.

STORY-TELLING

When a young child wants a story he may have in mind an old favourite, he may want a new one, or he may even specify a subject, saying "Tell me about the time that big dog came into our house" or "Tell me about the little girl who went to the hospital to have her tonsils out." If he wants an old favourite his story book is in the cardboard box. For a new one, improvise on boat trips, visits to his grandparents, stories of farm life or impromptu tales of foreign countries and far-away places.

Story books for children of this age should have interesting pictures and short simple texts. The most welcome themes are those dealing with the kind of life and experience that the child knows about. He must be able to put himself into the story. Stories of animals or other children are usually a good bet and simple humour is always appealing.

DRAMATIC PLAY

When children act out scenes and stories they are interpreting life to themselves. Games that involve doctor and nurse, or going to a hospital, are the child's effort to explore experience and to gain the reassurance that while a polio injection might prick a bit, it isn't really fatal.

The nurse kit comes into play again and again. The game of "house" or "shop" that occupies them in play at home also attracts their attention in a moving car. The child shows his urge to make-believe in his drawings, the simple songs he may invent, the stories he tells, but it is seen most clearly in his play-acting. That is why hand puppets, dressing-up clothes and toys suitable for imaginative play are so important to the young child.

Don't make the mistake of discouraging the child

from this kind of informal dramatic play by imposing adult standards of realism or saying "Don't be silly, Peter, you're a boy—you can't be mother." But at his age, he can. In his world of make-believe he can be anything he wants and all he expects of his parents is that they should be a good audience or supporting cast.

The very young child won't stick to one activity for very long, especially in a car. Give him a wide choice of things to do. See that his brothers and sisters encourage and help him when he needs it. A child of seven or eight is often quite skilled in helping a three- or four-year-old. The older child and the younger are close enough in age for their play interests to overlap, and the older child is mature enough not to fight with the younger for possession of toys or in competition for adult attention. The very young child won't be a perfect angel on any trip, but he can have a reasonably happy time of it.

One more thing needs to be said. On occasion, all you need to do to let children enjoy themselves in a car is to leave them alone. They have talents and inventiveness of their own, and if they are getting on well enough, leave well enough alone.

SAFETY HINTS FROM THE A.A.

When children are kept occupied with games and activities like those in this book, there is seldom need to worry about their safety. They are usually too busy to get into trouble.

Even so, children on long trips are bound to become fidgety and impatient at one time or another and small skirmishes will break out. If things get out of hand, a good idea is to pull off the road and declare a ten-minute break.

Children allowed to do as they like in a car can form a threefold threat to safety. They can hurt themselves by falling over the back of the seats or by being thrown against the dashboard in sudden stops; they can distract the driver long enough to send a car out of control; and they can distract the drivers of other cars around them.

Here are some suggestions that you might want to pass on to your children. Of course, the age of a child has much to do with the amount of supervision needed.

Do not sit in the driver's lap (it is surprising how often this is permitted).

Do not stand on seats or climb over them.

Do not play with the door handles or locks.

Do not stick arms, heads or toys out of car windows.

Do not play with large objects, like balloons or rubber swimming rings.

Do not carry sharp wood or metal objects.

Do not throw paper or rubbish out of the windows.

Do not fiddle with the car controls, such as the gear lever or ignition key.

No rough-house play.

Here are some general ideas on how to get the most out of travelling with your children.

Tell your children in advance where they are going. This will make them more interested in the trip and give them something to look forward to.

A well-planned travel schedule, allowing for short driving days with stops planned to coincide with the youngsters' eating and sleeping habits, will go a long way towards ensuring the most pleasure and enjoyment. Children can't sit still for long periods of time and will inevitably become irritable on long stages. Try buying only a few gallons of petrol at a time so that you stop more often at petrol stations, then it is often possible for everyone to get out and stretch their legs.

A flexible approach to the day's driving is another important factor. Don't be one of those drivers who has a strict schedule: he must go so many miles per day come what may, and he cannot eat until he reaches such and such a town. Better to stop when the fancy takes you.

Take with you plenty of fresh and dried fruit, but go easy with the sweets. A bottle or flask of water, fruit juice, squash or milk will be appreciated by everyone. Paper or plastic cups are best.

A picnic lunch is a welcome change to children. It gives them a chance to enjoy the outdoor surroundings and work off some of their surplus energy. Taking them to restaurants can be fun, too, although it does present problems occasionally. Older children find it a great experience, a chance to be grown up, and to try new and different types of food. Small fry need a little special handling: a restaurant can be just as confining to them as a car. Try to have your meals with children before the rush hours. You won't have to wait so long for service and the waitress will be able to give them added attention. Try not to alter their diet too much, either, but keep to dishes they are familiar with at home.

Dress children in comfortable, easily washed clothing.

Before going on a long trip with a small child, get him used to sleeping under different conditions beforehand. Sometimes sleeping elsewhere than his cot makes it easier for him to adjust to travelling. Carry a full day's supply of water in a thermos reserved for his use. Also consider taking a collapsible pushcart. It is a surprisingly versatile piece of equipment, increasing family mobility while sightseeing.

There always seems to be the problem of sticky hands and faces. Keep a damp cloth or face-flannel in a plastic bag in the glove box. It will keep moist all day. A packet of tissues is also very useful.

A small mattress can transform the back seat into a bed, and a pillow and blanket are essential.

Very often an insect repellent will come in handy and wherever you are going, don't forget to take a well-stocked first-aid box, looking it over first to see that the contents are all there and in good condition.

**LOOK AFTER
YOUR FAMILY
ON THE ROAD**

· · ·

**DRIVE
WITH CARE
AND
COURTESY**